Reference The Scripture

Daniel & Lynn,

Thank you for all
that you have done
for us. We love you.

James & Madlin

Reference The Scripture

A Scripture Reference

James Rhodes

Writers Club Press
New York Lincoln Shanghai

Reference The Scripture
A Scripture Reference

Writers Club Press
an imprint of iUniverse, Inc.

For information address:
iUniverse, Inc.
2021 Pine Lake Road, Suite 100
Lincoln, NE 68512
www.iuniverse.com

All scriptures are taken from the New King James Bible and the King James Bible

ISBN: 0-595-26507-3

Printed in the United States of America

Contents

INTRODUCTION xi

- *ABILITY* *1*
- *ABSTAIN* *3*
- *ABUNDANCE* *3*
- *ACCESS TO GOD* *4*
- *ACKNOWLEDGMENT* *6*
- *ADORNMENT* *7*
- *ADULTERY* *7*
- *ADVERSARIES* *8*
- *ADVERSITY* *10*
- *ADVOCATE* *11*
- *AFFLICTIONS* *12*
- *ANGELS* *14*
- *ANGER* *15*
- *ANXIETY* *17*
- *ASSURANCE* *18*
- *ATONEMENT* *20*
- *AUTHORITY* *21*
- *BEWARE* *24*
- *CHEERFULNESS* *24*
- *CHILDREN* *25*
- *CHRISTIANS* *25*
- *CHRISTIAN SINGLES* *34*
- *COMFORT* *36*
- *COMFORTER* *36*

- *COMMUNION* *37*
- *CONDEMNATION* *38*
- *CONFESSING CHRIST* *38*
- *CONFESSING SIN* *39*
- *CONFORMITY* *40*
- *CORRECTION* *40*
- *COUNSEL* *42*
- *DAMNATION* *44*
- *DEATH OF A CHRISTIAN* *44*
- *DESIRE* *45*
- *DISCIPLESHIP* *46*
- *DIVORCE* *47*
- *EDIFICATION* *48*
- *END TIME EVENTS* *49*
- *ENDURANCE* *51*
- *ETERNAL LIFE* *51*
- *FAITH IN GOD* *53*
- *FASTING* *56*
- *FAVOR* *57*
- *FEAR* *58*
- *FELLOWSHIP* *59*
- *FIRSTFRUITS* *62*
- *FORGIVENESS* *63*
- *FORNICATION* *65*
- *FRUIT OF THE WOMB* *66*
- *GOODNESS OF GOD* *67*
- *GOSSIP* *68*
- *HALLOWEEN* *69*
- *HEALING* *71*
- *HEAVEN* *73*
- *HELL* *75*

- *THE HOLY SPIRIT* *76*
- *HOMOSEXUALITY* *80*
- *HOROSCOPES* *80*
- *HUMILITY* *80*
- *JUDGMENT* *82*
- *LAZINESS* *85*
- *LOVE* *86*
- *LUST* *89*
- *MARRIAGE* *91*
- *PASTORS* *97*
- *PATIENCE* *100*
- *PEACE* *100*
- *PRAYER* *103*
- *THE PRESENCE OF GOD* *106*
- *PROMISED BLESSINGS OF OBEDIENCE* *108*
- *PROSPERITY* *109*
- *PROTECTION* *111*
- *THE RAPTURE* *114*
- *THE RESURRECTION* *117*
- *RIGHTEOUSNESS* *118*
- *SANCTIFICATION* *120*
- *SALVATION* *121*
- *SPEAKING IN TONGUES* *125*
- *SPIRIT OF THE ANTICHRIST* *126*
- *TATTOOS* *127*
- *TEMPTATION* *127*
- *TITHES AND OFFERINGS* *129*
- *THE TONGUE* *131*
- *TRUSTING GOD* *134*
- *WARFARE* *137*

Acknowledgments

I would like to thank God for giving me the ability, wisdom and knowledge to send His word forth using the personality which He blessed me with. And my Lord and Savior Jesus Christ for dying for me that I may live and allowing me to be forgiven for my sins.

My precious wife Madeline for allowing me to spend countless hours studying the word and preparing this book, and for encouraging me to continue on when I wanted to give up. Thank you Boo!

Pastor Orlando and Michelle Scott for loving me, encouraging me, and for always being there when I needed them the most. And for giving me a strong foundation in the word of God which allowed me to stand on my own and help others. Thank you.

The members of Courts of Praise Christian Fellowship who always believed in me even when I wasn't believing in myself. Especially Kenneth Howell who asked me personally and encouraged me to write this scripture reference. Anthony Milton who joined me in a prayer of agreement a few years ago that this might come to pass. And Clementine Davis who was more excited than I was when I spoke with her concerning my dreams of writing books. Thank you all for believing in me. "It's All About Him."

I would like to thank Dr Johnny L. and Lilliette Magee of the "Totally Blessed Ministry" of Full Assurance of Faith who opened the doors of the church as well as their home and welcomed my wife and I with open arms. Because of his teaching of the word of God I was able to complete this book and is a man to be followed, because he is a true follower of Christ. Being a part of Full Assurance of Faith was truly a life-changing event. Thank you for the impartation. And the members of Full Assurance who encouraged me, helped me, and rejoiced with me as they saw my dream coming to pass. Thank you all. Shalom

Christine Thorps for assisting me in editing, Shirrell Purnell for her scriptural input, and Parrish Purnell for putting together a cover for me. Thank you.

And of course, I have to thank my mother, Larine Rhodes who kept me in the church as a child, and trained me up the way that I should go. Who as a single parent made life seem so easy and never complained. Because she is a woman of God who prayed for her children, we were kept by the Lord. Thank you for instructing me as a child and encouraging me as an adult. Thanks again. I am truly blessed to have a mother like you.

INTRODUCTION

There have been times in my Christian walk that I was in search of a scripture, and could not find it. Therefore I spent much time searching the scriptures trying to find it.

So eventually I started writing them down and it was such a blessing to be able to find a scripture right now, right away. I am sure that this will be a blessing to others as well.

Others have asked questions about where to find certain subjects or topics concerning the word of God and this quick reference will help to get that right now word from God.

These topics have been arranged in alphabetical order and are subjects that Christians as well as the unsaved need to know and will help them live a victorious life in Christ.

ABILITY

Every man shall give as he is able, according to the blessing of the Lord thy God which he hath given thee. Deuteronomy 16:17

And Caleb stilled the people before Moses, and said, Let us go up at once, and possess it; for we are well able to overcome it. Numbers 13:30

For in many things we offend all. If any man offend not in word, the same is a perfect man, and able also to bridle the whole body. James 3:2

And being fully persuaded that, what he had promised, he was able also to perform. Romans 4:21

There hath no temptation taken you but such as is common to man: but God is faithful, who will not suffer you to be tempted above that ye are able; but will with the temptation also make a way to escape, that ye may be able to bear it. 1 Corinthians 10:13

Now I Nebuchadnezar praise and extol and honour the King of heaven, all whose works are truth, and his ways judgment: and those that walk in pride he is able to abase. Daniel 4:37

And God is able to make all grace abound toward you; that ye, always having all sufficiency in all things, may abound to every good work: 2 Corinthians 9:8

Now unto him that is able to do exceeding abundantly above all that we ask or think, according to the power that worketh in us, Ephesians 3:20

If any man speak, let him speak as the oracles of God; if any man minister, let him do it as of the ability which God giveth: that God in all things may be glorified through Jesus Christ, to whom be praise and dominion for ever and ever. Amen. 1 Peter 4:11

Now unto him that is able to keep you from falling, and to present you faultless before the presence of his glory with exceeding joy, Jude 24

For in that he himself hath suffered being tempted, he is able to succour them that are tempted. Hebrew 2:18

For we have not an high priest which cannot be touched with the feelings of our infirmities; but was in all points tempted like as we are, yet without sin. Hebrews 4:15

Wherefore he is able also to save them to the uttermost that come unto God by him, seeing he ever liveth to make intercession for them. Hebrew 7:25

For I will give you a mouth and wisdom, which all your adversaries shall not be able to gainsay nor resist. Luke 21:15

Put on the whole armour of God, that ye may be able to stand against the wiles of the devil. Ephesians 6:11

Wherefore take unto you the whole armour of God, that ye may be able to withstand in the evil day, and having done all, to stand. Ephesians 6:13

And Jesus looking upon them saith, With men it is impossible, but not with God: for with God all things are possible. Mark 10:27

I can do all things through Christ which strengtheneth me. Philippians 4:13

But my God shall supply all your need according to his riches in glory by Christ Jesus. Philippians 4:19

ABSTAIN

For this is the will of God, even your sanctification, that ye should abstain from fornication: 1 Thessalonians 4:3

Dearly beloved, I beseech you as strangers and pilgrims, abstain from fleshly lusts, which war against the soul; 1 Peter 2:11

Abstain from all appearance of evil. 1 Thessalonians 5:22

It is good neither to eat flesh, nor to drink wine, nor any thing whereby thy brother stumbleth, or is offended, or is made weak. Romans 14:21

ABUNDANCE

And Elijah said unto Ahab, Get thee up, eat and drink; for there is a sound of abundance of rain. 1 Kings 18:41

And the Lord passed by before him, and proclaimed, The Lord, The Lord God, merciful and gracious, longsuffering, and abundant in goodness and truth, Exodus 34:6

Behold, I will bring it health and cure, and I will cure them, and will reveal unto them the abundance of peace and truth. Jeremiah 33:6

Now unto him that is able to do exceeding abundantly above all that we ask or think, according to the power that worketh in us, Ephesians 3:20

And the grace of our Lord was exceeding abundant with faith and love which is in Christ Jesus. 1 Timothy 1:14

Blessed be the God and Father of our Lord Jesus Christ, which according to his abundant mercy hath begotten us again unto a lively hope by the resurrection of Jesus Christ from the dead, 1 Peter 1:3

In his days shall the righteous flourish; and abundance of peace so long as the moon endureth. Psalm 72:7

But the meek shall inherit the earth; and shall delight themselves in the abundance of peace. Psalm 37:11

Moreover the law entered, that the offence might abound. But where sin abounded, grace did much more abound: Romans 5:20

For whosoever hath, to him shall be given, and he shall have more abundance: but whosoever hath not, from him shall be taken away even that he hath. Matthew 13:12

The thief cometh not, but for to steal, and to kill, and to destroy: I am come that they might have life, and that they might have it more abundantly. John 10:10

ACCESS TO GOD

Jesus saith unto him, I am the way, the truth, and the life: no man cometh unto the Father, but by me. John 14:6

But now in Christ Jesus ye who sometimes were far off are made nigh by the blood of Christ. Ephesians 2:13

For through him we both have access by one Spirit unto the Father. Ephesians 2:18

And hath raised us up together, and made us sit together in heavenly places in Christ Jesus: Ephesians 2:6

Having predestinated us unto the adoption of children by Jesus Christ to himself, according to the good pleasure of his will, Ephesians 1:5

By whom also we have access by faith into this grace wherein we stand, and rejoice in hope of the glory of God. Romans 5:2

The Lord is nigh unto all them that call upon him, to all that call upon him in truth. Psalm 145:18

Draw nigh to God, and he will draw nigh to you. Cleanse your hands, ye sinners; and purify your hearts, ye doubled minded. James 4:8

Humble yourselves in the sight of the Lord, and he shall lift you up. James 4:10

Seeing then that we have a great high priest, that is passed into the heavens, Jesus the Son of God, let us hold fast our profession. Hebrews 4:14

For we have not an high priest which cannot be touched with the feelings of our infirmities; but was in all points tempted like as we are, yet without sin. Hebrews 4:15

Let us therefore come boldly unto the throne of grace, that we may obtain mercy, and find grace to help in time of need. Hebrews 4:16

According to the eternal purpose which he purposed in Christ Jesus our Lord:
In whom we have boldness and access with confidence by the faith of him. Ephesians 3:11-12

In the body of his flesh through death, to present you holy and unblameable and unreproveable in his sight: Colossians 1:22

And when they were come, and had gathered the church together, they rehearsed all that God had done with them, and how he had opened the door of faith unto the Gentiles. Acts 14:27

Wherefore he is able also to save them to the uttermost that come unto God by him, seeing he ever liveth to make intercession for them. Hebrews 7:25

ACKNOWLEDGMENT

I acknowledged my sin unto thee, and mine iniquity have I not hid. I said, I will confess my transgressions unto the Lord; and thou forgavest the iniquity of my sin. Selah. Psalms 32:5

For I acknowledge my transgressions: and my sin is ever before me. Psalms 51:3

In all thy ways acknowledge him, and he shall direct thy paths. Proverbs 3:6

Hear, ye that are far off, what I have done; and, ye that are near, acknowledge my might. Isaiah 33:13

And their seed shall be known among the Gentiles, and their offspring among the people: all that see them shall acknowledge them, that they are the seed which the Lord hath blessed. Isaiah 61:9

That their hearts might be comforted, being knit together in love, and unto all riches of the full assurance of understanding, to the acknowledgement of the mystery of God, and of the Father, and of Christ; Colossians 2:2

ADORNMENT

Bless the Lord, O my soul. O Lord my God, thou art very great; thou art clothed with honour and majesty. Psalm 104:1

Not purloining, but shewing all good fidelity; that they may adorn the doctrine of God our Saviour in all things. Titus 2:10

In like manner also, that women adorn themselves in modest apparel, with shamefacedness and sobriety; not with broided hair, or gold, or pearls, or costly array; 1 Timothy 2:9

Whose adorning let it not be that outward adorning of plaiting the hair, and of wearing of gold, or of putting on of apparel; 1 Peter 3:3

But let it be the hidden man of the heart, in that which is not corruptible, even the ornament of a meek and quiet spirit, which is in the sight of God of great price. 1 Peter 3:4

For after this manner in the old time the holy women also, who trusted in God, adorned themselves, being in subjection unto their own husbands: 1 Peter 3:5

ADULTERY

Thou shalt not commit adultery. Exodus 20:14

But I say unto you, That whosoever looketh on a woman to lust after her hath committed adultery with her already in his heart. Matthew 5:28

For her house inclineth unto death, and her paths unto the dead. Proverbs 2:18

So he that goeth into his neighbour's wife; whosoever toucheth her shall not be innocent. Proverbs 6:29

But whoso committeth adultery with a woman lacketh understanding: he that doeth it destroyeth his own soul. Proverbs 6:32

Whoso loveth wisdom rejoiceth his father: but he that keepeth company with harlots spendeth his substance. Proverbs 29:3

Such is the way of an adulterous woman; she eateth, and wipeth her mouth, and saith, I have done no wickedness. Proverbs 30:20

Her house is the way to hell, going down to the chambers of death. Proverbs 7:27

I wrote unto you in an epistle not to company with fornicators: 1 Corinthians 5:9

Know ye not that the unrighteous shall not inherit the kingdom of God? Be not deceived: neither fornicators, nor idolaters, nor adulterers, nor effeminate, nor abusers of themselves with mankind, 1 Corinthians 6:9

Marriage is honourable in all, and the bed undefiled: but whoremongers and adulterers God will judge. Hebrews 13:4

Moreover thou shalt not lie carnally with thy neighbor's wife, to defile thyself with her. Leviticus 18:20

ADVERSARIES

Be sober, be vigilant; because your adversary the devil, as a roaring lion, walketh about, seeking whom he may devour: 1 Peter 5:8

For a great door and effectual is opened unto me, and there are many adversaries. 1 Corinthians 16:9

And her adversary also provoked her sore, for to make her fret, because the Lord had shut up her womb.(HANNAH) 1 Samuel 1:6

So Balaam rose in the morning, saddled his donkey, and went with the princes of Moab.
Then God's anger was aroused because he went, and the Angel of the Lord took His stand in the way as an adversary against him. And he was riding on his donkey, and his two servants were with him. Numbers 22:21-22 NKJV

And the Lord stirred up an adversary unto Solomon, Hadad the Edomite: he was of the king's seed in Edom. 1 Kings 11:14

And God stirred him up another adversary, Rezon the son of Eliadah, which fled from his lord Hadadezer king of Zobah. 1 Kings 11:23

But I say unto you, Love your enemies, bless them that curse you, do good to them that hate you, and pray for them which despitefully use you, and persecute you; Matthew 5:44

For I will give you a mouth and wisdom, which all your adversaries shall not be able to gainsay nor resist. Luke 21:15

And in nothing terrified by your adversaries: which is to them an evident token of perdition, but to you of salvation, and that of God. Philippians 1:28

I will therefore that the younger women marry, bear children, guide the house, give none occasion to the adversary to speak reproachfully. 1 Timothy 5:14

But a certain fearful looking for of judgment and fiery indignation, which shall devour the adversaries. Hebrews 10:27

ADVERSITY

And unto Adam he said, Because thou hast hearkened unto the voice of thy wife, and hast eaten of the tree, of which I commanded thee, saying, Thou shalt not eat of it: cursed is the ground for thy sake; in sorrow shalt thou eat of it all the days of thy life; Genesis 3:17

And if ye shall despise my statutes, or if your soul abhor my judgments, so that ye will not do all my commandments, but that ye break my covenant: I also will do this unto you; I will even appoint over you terror, consumption, and the burning ague, that shall consume the eyes, and cause sorrow of heart: and ye shall sow your seed in vain, for your enemies shall eat it. Leviticus 26:15-16

And thou shalt remember all the way which the Lord thy God led thee these forty years in the wilderness, to humble thee, and to prove thee, to know what was in thine heart, whether thou wouldest keep his commandments, or no. Deuteronomy 8:2

That the trial of your faith, being much more precious than of gold that perisheth, though it be tried with fire, might be found unto praise and honour and glory at the appearing of Jesus Christ: 1 Peter 1:7

That thou mayest give him rest from the days of adversity, until the pit be digged for the wicked. Psalm 94:13

If thou faint in the day of adversity; thy strength is small. Proverbs 24:10

My brethren, count it all joy when ye fall into divers temptations; James 1:2

But when they in their trouble did turn unto the Lord God of Israel, and sought him, he was found of them. 2 Chronicles 15:4

And not only so, but we glory in tribulations also: knowing that tribulation worketh patience; Romans 5:3

ADVOCATE

In whom we have redemption through his blood, the forgiveness of sins, according to the riches of his grace; Ephesians 1:7

For he hath made him to be sin for us, who knew no sin; that we might be made the righteousness of God in him. 2 Corinthians 5:21

But I have prayed for thee, that thy faith fail not: and when thou art converted, strengthen thy brethren. Luke 22:32

So that we may boldly say, The Lord is my helper, and I will not fear what man shall do unto me. Hebrews 13:6

The Lord is my shepherd; I shall not want. Psalm 23:1

And I give unto them eternal life; and they shall never perish, neither shall any man pluck them out of my hand. John 10:28

Notwithstanding the Lord stood with me, and strengthened me; that by me the preaching might be fully known, and that all the Gentiles might hear: and I was delivered out of the mouth of the lion. 2 Timothy 4:17

And the Lord shall deliver me from every evil work, and will preserve me unto his heavenly kingdom: to whom be glory for ever and ever. Amen. 2 Timothy 4:18

And I will pray the Father, and he shall give you another Comforter, that he may abide with you for ever; John 14:16

My little children, these things write I unto you, that ye sin not. And if any man sin, we have an advocate with the Father, Jesus Christ the righteous: 1 John 2:1

Who is he that condemneth? It is Christ that died, yea rather, that is risen again, who is even at the right hand of God, who also maketh intercession for us. Romans 8:34

For Christ is not entered into the holy places made with hands, which are the figures of the true; but into heaven itself, now to appear in the presence of God for us. Hebrews 9:24

AFFLICTIONS

I will go and return to my place, till they acknowledge their offence, and seek my face: in their affliction they will seek me early. Hosea 5:15

Fools because of their transgression, and because of their iniquities, are afflicted. Psalm 107:17

Before I was afflicted I went astray: but now have I kept thy word. Psalm 119:67

And when he was in affliction, he besought the Lord his God, and humbled himself greatly before the God of his fathers, 2 Chronicles 33:12

Behold, I have refined thee, but not with silver; I have chosen thee in the furnace of affliction. Isaiah 48:10

And have no root in themselves, and so endure but for a time: afterward, when affliction or persecution ariseth for the word's sake, immediately they are offended. Mark 4:17

Then shall they deliver you up to be afflicted, and shall kill you: and ye shall be hated of all nations for my name's sake. Matthew 24:9

But watch thou in all things, endure afflictions, do the work of an evangelist, make full proof of thy ministry. 2 Timothy 4:5

And ye became followers of us, and of the Lord, having received the word in much affliction, with joy of the Holy Ghost: 1 Thessalonians 1:6

That no man should be moved by these afflictions: for yourselves know that we are appointed thereunto. 1 Thessalonians 3:3

Persecutions, afflictions, which came unto me at Antioch, at Iconium, at Lystra; what persecutions I endured: but out of them all the Lord delivered me. 2 Timothy 3:11

For our light affliction, which is but for a moment, worketh for us a far more exceeding and eternal weight of glory; 2 Corinthians 4:17

We are troubled on every side, yet not distressed; we are perplexed, but not in despair;
Persecuted, but not forsaken; cast down, but not destroyed; 2 Corinthians 4:8,9

Who shall separate us from the love of Christ? Shall tribulation, or distress, or persecution, or famine, or nakedness, or peril or sword? Romans 8:35

Many are the afflictions of the righteous: but the Lord delivereth him out of them all. Psalm 34:19

Is any among of you afflicted? Let him pray. Is any merry? Let him sing Psalms. James 5:13

And to you who are troubled rest with us, when the Lord Jesus shall be revealed from heaven with his mighty angels, 2 Thessalonians 1:7

ANGELS

For I will defend this city, to save it, for mine own sake, and for my servant David's sake.

And it came to pass that night, that the angel of the Lord went out, and smote in the camp of the Assyrians an hundred fourscore and five thousand: and when they arose early in the morning, behold, they were all dead corpses. 2 Kings 19:34,35

And when the servant of the man of God was risen early, and gone forth, behold, an host compassed the city both with horses and chariots. And his servant said unto him, Alas, my master! How shall we do? And he answered, Fear not: for they that be with us are more than they that be with them.

And Elisha prayed, and said, Lord, I pray thee, open his eyes, that he may see. And the Lord opened the eyes of the young man; and he saw: and, behold, the mountain was full of horses and chariots of fire round about Elisha. 2 Kings 6:15-17

The Lord of hosts is with us; the God of Jacob is our refuge. Selah. Psalm 46:11

The chariots of God are twenty thousand, even thousands of angels: the Lord is among them, as in Sinai, in the holy place. Psalm 68:17

Bless the Lord, ye his angels, that excel in strength, that do his commandments, hearkening unto the voice of his word.

Bless ye the Lord, all ye his hosts; ye ministers of his, that do his pleasure. Psalm 103:20,21

Then said I, Woe is me! For I am undone; because I am a man of unclean lips: and I dwell in the midst of a people of unclean lips, for mine eyes have seen the King, the Lord of hosts. Isaiah 6:5

Take heed that ye despise not one of these little ones; for I say unto you, That in heaven their angels do always behold the face of my Father which is in heaven. Matthew 18:10

Thinkest thou that I cannot now pray to my Father, and he shall presently give me more than twelve legions of angels? Matthew 26:53

And as Asaias said before, except the Lord of Sabaoth had left us a seed, we had been as Sodoma, and been made like unto Gomorrha. Romans 9:29

Are they not all ministering spirits, sent forth to minister for them who shall be heirs of salvation? Hebrews 1:14

Be ye are come unto mount Sion, and unto the city of the living God, the heavenly Jerusalem, and to an innumerable company of angels, Hebrews 12:22

Be not forgetful to entertain strangers: for thereby some have entertained angels unawares. Hebrews 13:2

Behold, the hire of the labourers who have reaped down your fields, which is of you kept back by fraud, crieth: and the cries of them which have reaped are enterd into the ears of the Lord of sabaoth. James 5:4

ANGER

Be ye angry, and sin not: let not the sun go down upon your wrath. Ephesians 4:26

Let all bitterness, and wrath, and anger, and clamour, and evil speaking, be put away from you, with all malice. Ephesians 4:31

For his anger endureth but a moment; in his favour is life: weeping may endure for a night, but joy cometh in the morning. Psalm 30:5

Who is a God like unto thee, that pardoneth iniquity, and passeth by the transgression of the remnant of his heritage? He retaineth not his anger forever, because he delighteth in mercy. Micah 7:18

The fear of a king is as the roaring of a lion: whoso provoketh him to anger sinneth against his own soul. Proverbs 20:2

A man of great wrath shall suffer punishment: for if thou deliver him, yet thou must do it again. Proverbs 19:19

He that is slow to wrath is of great understanding: but he that is hasty of spirit exalteth folly. Proverbs 14:29

A soft answer turneth away wrath: but grievous words stir up anger. Proverbs 15:1

A gift in secret pacifieth anger: and a reward in the bosom strong wrath. Proverbs 21:14

The discretion of a man deferreth his anger; and it is his glory to pass over a transgression. Proverbs 19:11

A wrathful man stirreth up strife: but he that is slow to anger, appeaseth strife. Proverbs 15:18

The king's favour is toward a wise servant: but his wrath is against him that causeth shame. Proverbs 14:35

Wherefore, my beloved brethren, let every man be swift to hear, slow to speak, slow to wrath. James 1:19

For the wrath of man worketh not the righteousness of God. James 1:20

And the servant of the Lord must not strive; but be gentle unto all men, apt to teach, patient, 2 Timothy 2:24

Fathers, provoke not your children to anger, lest they be discouraged. Colossians 3:21

ANXIETY

Fret not thyself because of evildoers, neither be thou envious against the workers of iniquity. Psalm 37:1

Rest in the Lord, and wait patiently for him: fret not thyself because of him who prospereth in his way, because of the man who bringeth wicked devices to pass. Psalm 37:7

But the meek shall inherit the earth; and shall delight themselves in the abundance of peace. Psalm 37:11

Therefore I say unto you, Take no thought for your life, what ye shall eat, or what ye shall drink; nor yet for your body, what ye shall put on. Is not the life more than meat, and the body than raiment?
Behold the fowls of the air: for they sow not, neither do they reap, nor gather into barns; yet your heavenly Father feedeth them. Are ye not much better than they?
Matthew 6:25,26
(For after all these things do the Gentiles seek:) for your heavenly Father knoweth that ye have need of all these things.
But seek ye first the kingdom of God, and his righteousness; and all these things shall be added unto you. Matthew 6:32,33

Come unto me, all ye that labour and are heavy laden, and I will give you rest. Matthew 11:28

He also that received seed among the thorns is he that heareth the word; and the care of this world, and the deceitfulness of riches, choke the word, and he becometh unfruitful. Matthew 13:22

And we know that all things work together for good to them that love God, to them who are the called according to his purpose. Romans 8:28

Be careful for nothing; but in every thing by prayer and supplication with thanksgiving let your requests be made known unto God. Philippians 4:6

Casting all your care upon him; for he careth for you. 1 Peter 5:7

ASSURANCE

According as he hath chosen us in him before the foundation of the world, that we should be holy and without blame before him in love: Having predestinated us unto the adoption of children by Jesus Christ to himself, according to the good pleasure of his will, Ephesians 1:4,5

In whom we have redemption through his blood, the forgiveness of sins, according to the riches of his grace; Ephesians 1:7

In whom also we have obtained an inheritance, being predestinated according to the purpose of him who worketh all things after the counsel of his own will: Ephesians 1:11

In whom ye also trusted, after that ye heard the word of truth, the gospel of your salvation: in whom also after that ye believed, ye were sealed with that holy Spirit of promise,
Which is the earnest of our inheritance until the redemption of the purchased possession, unto the praise of his glory. Ephesians 1:13,14

Verily, verily, I say unto you, He that heareth my word, and believeth on him that sent me, hath everlasting life, and shall not come into condemnation; but is passed from death unto life. John 5:24

These things have I written unto you that believe on the name of the Son of God; that ye may know that ye have eternal life, and that ye may believe on the name of the Son of God. 1 John 5:13

And I give unto them eternal life; and they shall never perish, neither shall any man pluck them out of my hand. John 10:28

The Spirit itself beareth witness with our spirit, that we are the children of God: Romans 8:16

And if children, then heirs; heirs of God, and joint-heirs with Christ; if so be that we suffer with him, that we may be also glorified together. Romans 8:17

And we know that all things work together for good to them that love God, to them who are the called according to his purpose. Romans 8:28

What shall we then say to these things? If God be for us, who can be against us? Romans 8:31

Who shall lay any thing to the charge of God's elect? It is God that justifieth. Romans 8:33

Who is he that condemneth? It is Christ that died, yea rather, that is risen again, who is even at the right hand of God, who also maketh intercession for us. Romans 8:34

Who shall separate us from the love of Christ? Shall tribulation, or distress, or persecution, or famine, or nakedness, or peril, or sword? Romans 8:35

For I am persuaded, that neither death, nor life, nor angels, nor principalities, nor powers, nor things present, nor things to come,
Nor height, nor depth, nor any other creature, shall be able to separate

us from the love of God, which is in Christ Jesus our Lord. Romans 8:38,39

Being confident of this very thing, that he which hath begun a good work in you will perform it until the day of Jesus Christ: Philippians 1:6

But my God shall supply all your need according to his riches in glory by Christ Jesus. Philippians 4:19

For all the promises of God in him are yea, and in him Amen, unto the glory of God by us. 2 Corinthians 1:20

ATONEMENT

Therefore will I divide him a portion with the great, and he shall divide the spoil with the strong; because he hath poured out his soul unto death: and he was numbered with the transgressors; and he bare the sin of many, and made intercession for the transgressors. Isaiah 53:12

Neither by the blood of goats and calves, but by his own blood he entered in once into the holy place, having obtained eternal redemption for us. Hebrews 9:12

For he hath made him to be sin for us, who knew no sin; that we might be made the righteousness of God in him. 2 Corinthians 5:21

And such were some of you: but ye are washed, but ye are sanctified, but ye are justified in the name of the Lord Jesus, and by the Spirit of our God. 1 Corinthians 6:11

Blessed is he who transgression is forgiven, whose sin is covered. Psalm 32:1

For Christ is the end of the law for righteousness to everyone that believeth. Romans 10:4

Being justified freely by his grace through the redemption that is in Christ Jesus: Romans 3:24

Forasmuch as ye know that ye were not redeemed with corruptible things, as silver and gold, from your vain conversation received by tradition from your fathers;
But with the precious blood of Christ as of a lamb without blemish and without spot: 1 Peter 1:18,19

To wit, that God was in Christ, reconciling the world unto himself, not imputing their trespasses unto them; and hath committed unto us the word of reconciliation. 2 Corinthians 5:19

But if we walk in the light, as he is in the light, we have fellowship one with another, and the blood of Jesus Christ his Son cleanseth us from all sin. 1 John 1:7

AUTHORITY

For unto us a child is born, unto us a son is given: and the government shall be upon his shoulder: and his name shall be called Wonderful, Counsellor, The mighty God, The everlasting Father, The Prince of Peace. Isaiah 9:6

And she shall bring forth a son, and thou shalt call his name JESUS: for he shall save his people from their sins. Matthew 1:21

And Jesus came and spake unto them, saying, All power is given unto me in heaven and in earth. Matthew 28:18

And these signs shall follow them that believe; In my name shall they cast out devils; they shall speak with new tongues;
They shall take up serpents; and if they drink any deadly thing, it shall not hurt them; they shall lay hands on the sick, and they shall recover. Mark 16:17,18

He shall be great, and shall be called the Son of the Highest: and the Lord God shall give unto him the throne of his father David: Luke 1:32

Then he called his twelve disciples together, and gave them power and authority over all devils, and to cure diseases.
And he sent them to preach the kingdom of God, and to heal the sick. Luke 9:1,2

And the seventy returned again with joy, saying, Lord, even the devils are subject unto us through thy name. Luke 10:17

Behold, I give unto you power to tread on serpents and scorpions, and over all the power of the enemy: and nothing shall by any means hurt you. Luke 10:19

But as many as received him, to them gave he power to become the sons of God, even to them that believe on his name: John 1:12

The next day John seeth Jesus coming unto him, and saith, Behold the Lamb of God, which taketh away the sin of the world. John 1:29

Verily, verily, I say unto you, He that believeth on me, the works that I do shall he do also; and greater works than these shall he do because I go unto my Father. John 14:12

Let every soul be subject unto the higher powers. For there is no power but of God: the powers that be are ordained of God.
Whosoever therefore resisteth the power, resisteth the ordinance of God: and they that resist shall receive to themselves damnation.
For rulers are not a terror to good works, but to the evil. Wilt thou then not be afraid of the power? Do that which is good, and thou shalt have praise of the same:
For he is the minister of God to thee for good. But if thou do that which is evil, be afraid; for he beareth not the sword in vain: for he is

the minister of God, a revenger to execute wrath upon him that doeth evil. Romans 13:1-4

And they were all amazed, insomuch that they questioned among themselves, saying, What thing is this? What new doctrine is this? For with authority commandeth he even the unclean spirits, and they do obey him. Mark 1:27

For he taught them as one having authority, and not as the scribes. Matthew 7:29

But that ye may know that the Son of man hath power upon earth to forgive sins, (he said unto the sick of the palsy,) I say unto thee, Arise, and take up thy couch, and go into thine house. Luke 5:24

And he hath given him authority to execute judgment also, because he is the Son of man. John 5:27

Let as many servants as are under the yoke count their own masters worthy of all honour, that the name of God and his doctrine be not blasphemed. 1 Timothy 6:1

When the righteous are in authority, the people rejoice: but when the wicked beareth rule, the people mourn. Proverbs 29:2

For the earth is the Lord's, and the fulness thereof. 1 Corinthians 10:26

Wherefore God also hath highly exalted him, and given him a name which is above every name:
That at the name of Jesus every knee should bow, of things in heaven, and things in earth, and things under the earth; Philippians 2:9,10

And that every tongue should confess that Jesus Christ is Lord, to the glory of God the Father. Philippians 2:11

BEWARE

Now therefore beware, I pray thee, and drink not wine nor strong drink, and eat not any unclean thing: Judges 13:4

Beware of false prophets, which come to you in sheep's clothing, but inwardly they are ravening wolves. Matthew 7:15

And he said unto them, Take heed, and beware of covetousness: for a man's life consisteth not in the abundance of the things which he possesseth. Luke 12:15

Beware of dogs, beware of evil workers, beware of the concision. Philippians 3:2

Then beware lest thou forget the Lord, which brought thee forth out of the land of Egypt, from the house of bondage. Deuteronomy 6:12

Ye therefore, beloved, seeing ye know these things before, beware lest ye also, being led away with the error of the wicked, fall from your own stedfastness. 2 Peter 3:17

CHEERFULNESS

A merry heart maketh a cheerful countenance: but by sorrow of the heart the spirit is broken. Proverbs 15:13

Every man according as he purposeth in his heart, so let him give; not grudgingly, or of necessity: for God loveth a cheerful giver. 2 Corinthians 9:7

Or he that exhorteth, on exhortation: he that giveth, let him do it with simplicity; he that ruleth, with diligence; he that sheweth mercy, with cheerfulness. Romans 12:8

CHILDREN

Children, obey your parents in the Lord: for this is right.
Honour thy father and mother; (which is the first commandment with promise;)
That it may be well with thee, and thou mayest live long on the earth. Ephesians 6:1-3

And he lifted up his eyes, and saw the women and the children; and said, Who are those with thee? And he said, The children which God has graciously given thy servant. Genesis 33:5

Lo, children are an heritage of the Lord: and the fruit of the womb is his reward. Psalm 127:3

Children's children are the crown of old men; and the glory of children are their fathers. Proverbs 17:6

My son, hear the instruction of thy father, and forsake not the law of thy mother: Proverbs 1:8

Remember now thy Creator in the days of thy youth, while the evil days come not, nor the years draw nigh, when thou shalt say, I have no pleasure in them; Ecclesiastes 12:1

Children, obey your parents in all things: for this is well pleasing unto the Lord. Colossians 3:20

CHRISTIANS

…And the disciples were called Christians first at Antioch. Acts 11:26

For thou art an holy people unto the Lord thy God, and the Lord hath chosen thee to be a peculiar people unto himself, above all the nations that are upon the earth. Deuteronomy 14:2

Blessed is the man that walketh not in the counsel of the ungodly, nor standeth in the way of sinners, nor sitteth in the seat of the scornful.
But his delight is in the law of the Lord; and in his law doth he meditate day and night.
And he shall be like a tree planted by the rivers of water, that bringeth forth his fruit in his season; his leaf also shall not whither; and whatsoever he doeth shall prosper. Psalm 1:1-3

The Lord is my shepherd; I shall not want. Psalm 23:1

Give unto the Lord the glory due unto his name; worship the Lord in the beauty of holiness. Psalm 29:2

Thy word have I hid in mine heart, that I might not sin against thee. Psalm 119:11

Thy word is a lamp unto my feet, and a light unto my path. Psalm 119:105

Praise ye the Lord, Sing unto the Lord a new song, and his praise in the congregation of saints. Psalm 149:1

My son, forget not my law; but let thine heart keep my commandments:
For length of days, and long life, and peace, shall they add to thee. Proverbs 3:1,2

Be not wise in thine own eyes: fear the Lord, and depart from evil. Proverbs 3:7

Commit thy works unto the Lord, and thy thoughts shall be established. Proverbs 16:3

But he answered and said, It is written, Man shall not live by bread alone, but by every word that proceedeth out of the mouth of God. Matthew 4:4

But seek ye first the kingdom of God, and his righteousness; and all these things shall be added unto you. Matthew 6:33

But lay up for yourselves treasures in heaven, where neither moth nor rust doth corrupt, and where thieves do not break through nor steal: Matthew 6:20

Not everyone that saith unto me, Lord, Lord, shall enter into the kingdom of heaven; but he that doeth the will of my Father which is in heaven. Matthew 7:21

Verily I say unto you, Whatsoever ye shall bind on earth shall be bound in heaven: and whatsoever ye shall loose on earth shall be loosed in heaven.
Again I say unto you, That if two of you shall agree on earth as touching any thing that they shall ask, it shall be done for them of my Father which is in heaven.
For where two or three are gathered together in my name, there am I in the midst of them. Matthew 18:18-20

But he that is greatest among you shall be your servant. Matthew 23:11

And Jesus said unto him, No man, having put his hand to the plough, and looking back, is fit for the kingdom of God. Luke 9:62

Notwithstanding in this rejoice not, that the spirits are subject unto you; but rather rejoice, because your names are written in the heaven. Luke 10:20

But he said, Yea rather, blessed are they that hear the word of God, and keep it. Luke 11:28

Strive to enter in at the straight gate: for many, I say unto you, will seek to enter in, and shall not be able. Luke 13:24

God is a Spirit: and they that worship him must worship him in spirit and in truth. John 4:24

Jesus saith unto them, My meat is to do the will of him that sent me, and to finish his work. John 4:34

Afterward Jesus findeth him in the temple, and said unto him, Behold, thou art made whole: sin no more, lest a worse thing come unto thee. John 5:14

Then spake Jesus again unto them, saying, I am the light of the world: he that followeth me shall not walk in darkness, but shall have the light of life. John 8:12

Let your light so shine before men, that they may see your good works, and glorify your Father which is in heaven. Matthew 5:16

And ye shall know the truth, and the truth shall make you free. John 8:32

Let not you heart be troubled: ye believe in God, believe also in me. John 14:1

Verily, verily, I say unto you, He that believeth on me, the works that I do shall he do also; and greater works than these shall he do; because I go unto my Father . John 14:12

If ye shall ask anything in my name, I will do it. John 14:14

I am the vine, ye are the branches: He that abideth in me, and I in him, the same bringeth forth much fruit: for without me ye can do nothing. John 15:5

Jesus saith unto him, Thomas, because thou hast seen me, thou hast believed: blessed are they that have not seen, and yet have believed. John 20:29

(As it is written, I have made thee a father of many nations,) before him whom he believed, even God, who quickeneth the dead, and calleth those things which be not as though they were. Romans 4:17

Therefore we are buried with him by baptism into death: that like as Christ was raised up from the dead by the glory of the Father, even so we also should walk in newness of life. Romans 6:4

For if we have been planted together in the likeness of his death, we shall be also in the likeness of his resurrection: Romans 6:5

Knowing this, that our old man is crucified with him, that the body of sin might be destroyed, that henceforth we should not serve sin.
For he that is dead is freed from sin. Romans 6:6,7

So then they that are in the flesh cannot please God. Romans 8:8

For as many as are led by the Spirit of God, they are the sons of God. Romans 8:14

I beseech you therefore, brethren, by the mercies of God, that ye present your bodies a living sacrifice, holy, acceptable unto God, which is your reasonable service. Romans 12:1

And be not conformed to this world: but be ye transformed by the renewing of your mind, that ye may prove what is that good, and acceptable, and perfect, will of God. Romans12:2

Bless them which persecute you: bless, and curse not. Romans 12:14

Rejoice with them that do rejoice, and weep with them that weep. Romans 12:15

Recompense to no man evil for evil. Provide things honest in the sight of all men. Romans 12:17

Be not overcome of evil, but overcome evil with good. Romans 12:21

The night is far spent, the day is at hand: let us therefore cast off the works of darkness, and let us put on the armour of light. Romans 13:12

And that, knowing the time, that now it is high time to awake out of sleep: for now is our salvation nearer than when we believed. Romans 13:11

That your faith should not stand in the wisdom of men, but in the power of God. 1 Corinthians 2:5

For we are labourers together with God: ye are God's husbandry, ye are God's building. 1 Corinthians 3:9

For other foundation can no man lay than that is laid, which is Jesus Christ. 1 Corinthians 3:11

Know ye not that ye are the temple of God, and that the Spirit of God dwelleth in you? 1 Corinthians 3:16

If any man defile the temple of God, him shall God destroy; for the temple of God is holy, which temple ye are. 1 Corinthians 3:17

What? Know ye not that your body is the temple of the Holy Ghost which is in you, which ye have of God, and ye are not your own? 1 Corinthians 6:19

For God is not the author of confusion, but of peace, as in all churches of the saints. 1 Corinthians 14:33

Let all things be done decently and in order. 1 Corinthians 14:40

(For we walk by faith, not by sight:) 2 Corinthians 5:7

Therefore if any man be in Christ, he is a new creature: old things are passed away; behold, all things are become new. 2 Corinthians 5:17

Be ye not unequally yoked together with unbelievers: for what fellowship hath righteousness with unrighteousness? And what communion hath light with darkness? 2 Corinthians 6:14

I am crucified with Christ: nevertheless I live; yet not I, but Christ liveth in me: and the life which I now live in the flesh I live by the faith of the Son of God, who loved me, and gave himself for me. Galatians 2:20

There is neither Jew nor Greek, there is neither bond nor free, there is neither male nor female: for ye are all one in Christ Jesus. Galatians 3:28

And if ye be Christ's, then are ye Abraham's seed, and heirs according to the promise. Galatians 3:29

Now I say, That the heir, as long as he is a child, differeth nothing from a servant, though he be lord of all; Galatians 4:1

If we live in the Spirit, let us also walk in the Spirit. Galatians 5:25

Let us not be desirous of vain glory, provoking one another, envying one another. Galatians 5:26

Be not deceived; God is not mocked: for whatsoever a man soweth, that shall he also reap. Galatians 6:7

For he that soweth to his flesh shall of the flesh reap corruption; but he that soweth to the Spirit shall of the Spirit reap life everlasting. Galatians 6:8

And let us not be weary in well doing: for in due season we shall reap, if we faint not. Galatians 6:9

As we have therefore opportunity, let us do good unto all men, especially unto them that are of the household of faith. Galatians 6:10

And be not drunk with wine, wherein is excess; but be filled with the Spirit; Ephesians 5:18

For ye were sometimes darkness, but now are ye light in the Lord: walk as children of light: Ephesians 5:8

Wherefore be ye not unwise, but understanding what the will of the Lord is. Ephesians 5:17

Wherefore, my beloved, as ye have always obeyed, not as in my presence only, but now much more in my absence, work out your own salvation with fear and trembling. Philippians 2:12

Do all things without murmurings and disputings: Philippians 2:14

I can do all things through Christ which strengtheneth me. Philippians 4:13

But my God shall supply all your need according to his riches in glory by Christ Jesus. Philippians 4:19

Set your affection on things above, not on things on the earth. Colossians 3:2

And whatsoever ye do, do it heartily, as to the Lord, and not unto men; Colossians 3:23

For God hath not called us unto uncleanness, but unto holiness. 1 Thessalonians 4:7

In everything give thanks: for this is the will of God in Christ Jesus concerning you. 1 Thessalonians 5:18

Study to shew thyself approved unto God, a workman that needeth not to be ashamed, rightly dividing the word of truth. 2 Timothy 2:15

And the servant of the Lord must not strive; but be gentle unto all men, apt to teach, patient, 2 Timothy 2:24

Yea, and all that will live godly in Christ Jesus shall suffer persecution. 2 Timothy 3:12

To speak evil of no man, to be no brawlers, but gentle, shewing all meekness unto all men. Titus 3:2

But be ye doers of the word, and not hearers only, deceiving your own selves. James 1:22

Submit yourselves therefore to God. Resist the devil, and he will flee from you. James 4:7

Therefore to him that knoweth to do good, and doeth it not, to him it is sin. James 4:17

Because it is written, Be ye holy; for I am holy. 1 Peter 1:16

But ye are a chosen generation, a royal priesthood, an holy nation, a peculiar people; that ye should shew forth the praises of him who hath called you out of darkness into his marvelous light: 1 Peter 2:9

Submit yourselves to every ordinance of man for the Lord's sake: whether it be to the king, as supreme; 1 Peter 2:13

Remember ye not the former things, neither consider the things of old. Behold, I will do a new thing; now it shall spring forth; shall ye not know it? I will even make a way in the wilderness, and rivers in the desert. Isaiah 43:18,19

If there come any unto you, and bring not this doctrine, receive him not into your house, neither bid him God speed: 2 John 10

Ye are of God, little children, and have overcome them: because greater is he that is in you, than he that is in the world. 1 John 4:4

CHRISTIAN SINGLES

For the commandment is a lamp; and the law is light; and reproofs of instruction are the way of life:
To keep thee from the evil woman, from the flattery of the tongue of a strange woman.
Lust not after her beauty in thine heart; neither let her take thee with her eyelids.
For by means of a whorish woman a man is brought to a piece of bread: and the adulteress will hunt for the precious life. Proverbs 6:23-26

Can a man take fire in his bosom, and his clothes not be burned?
Can one go upon hot coals, and his feet not be burned?
Proverbs 6:27,28

Favour is deceitful, and beauty is vain: but a woman that feareth the Lord, she shall be praised. Proverbs 31:30

Except the Lord build the house, they labour in vain that build it: except the Lord keep the city, the watchman waketh but in vain. Psalm 127:1

But I say unto you, That whosoever looketh on a woman to lust after her hath committed adultery with her already in his heart. Matthew 5:28

I beseech you therefore, brethren, by the mercies of God, that ye present your bodies a living sacrifice, holy, acceptable unto God, which is your reasonable service. Romans 12:1

And be not conformed to this world: but be ye transformed by the renewing of your mind, that ye may prove what is that good, and acceptable, and perfect, will of God. Romans 12:2

Meats for the belly, and the belly for meats: but God shall destroy both it and them. Now the body is not for fornication, but for the Lord; and the Lord for the body. 1 Corinthians 6:13

Know ye not that your bodies are members of Christ? Shall I then take the members of Christ, and make them members of an harlot? God forbid. 1 Corinthians 6:15

What? Know ye not that he which is joined to an harlot is one body? For two, saith he, shall be one flesh. 1 Corinthians 6:16

Flee fornication. Every sin that a man doeth is without the body; but he that committeth fornication sinneth against his own body. 1 Corinthians 6:18

Art thou bound unto a wife? Seek not to be loosed. Art thou loosed from a wife? Seek not a wife. 1 Corinthians 7:27

There is difference also between a wife and a virgin. The unmarried woman careth for the things of the Lord, that she may be holy both in body and in spirit: but she that is married careth for the things of the world, how she may please her husband. 1 Corinthians 7:34

For this is the will of God, even your sanctification, that ye should abstain from fornication :
That every one of you should know how to possess his vessel in sanctification and honour; 1 Thessalonians 4:3,4

Marriage is honourable in all, and the bed undefiled: but whoremongers and adulterers God will judge. Hebrews 13:4

Blessed is the man that endureth temptation: for when he is tried, he shall receive the crown of life, which the Lord hath promised to them that love him. James 1:12

COMFORT

Blessed be God, even the Father of our Lord Jesus Christ, the Father of mercies, and the God of all comfort;
Who comforteth us in all our tribulation, that we may be able to comfort them which are in any trouble, by the comfort wherewith we ourselves are comforted of God. 2 Corinthians 1:3-4

Then had the churches rest throughout all Judaea and Galilee and Samaria, and were edified; and walking in the fear of the Lord, and in the comfort of the Holy Ghost, were multiplied. Acts 9:31

For whatsoever things were written aforetime were written for our learning, that we through patience and comfort of the scriptures might have hope. Romans 15:4

Nevertheless God, that comforteth those that are cast down, comforted us by the coming of Titus. 2 Corinthians 7:6

So that contrariwise ye ought rather to forgive him, and comfort him, lest perhaps such a one should be swallowed up with overmuch sorrow. 2 Corinthians 2:7

Now we exhort you, brethren, warn them that are unruly, comfort the feeble-minded, support the weak, be patient toward all men. 1 Thessalonians 5:14

COMFORTER

And I will pray the Father, and he shall give you another Comforter, that he may abide with you for ever; John 14:16

But the Comforter, which is the Holy Ghost, whom the Father will send in my name, he shall teach you all things, and bring all things to your remembrance, whatsoever I have said unto you. John 14:26

But when the Comforter is come, whom I will send unto you from the Father, even the Spirit of truth, which proceedeth from the Father, he shall testify of me: John 15:26

Nevertheless I tell you the truth; It is expedient for you that I go away; for if I go not away, the Comforter will not come unto you; but if I depart, I will send him unto you. John 16:7

Howbeit when he, the Spirit of truth, is come, he will guide you into all truth: for he shall not speak of himself; but whatsoever he shall hear, that shall he speak: and he will shew you things to come.
He shall glorify me: for he shall receive of mine, and shall shew it unto you. John 16:13,14

COMMUNION

And when he had given thanks, he brake it, and said, Take, eat: this is my body, which is broken for you: this do in remembrance of me.
After the same manner also he took the cup, when he had supped, saying, This cup is the new testament in my blood: this do ye, as oft as ye drink it, in remembrance of me.
For as often as ye eat this bread, and drink this cup, ye do shew the Lord's death till he come.
Wherefore whosoever shall eat this bread, and drink this cup of the Lord, unworthily, shall be guilty of the body and blood of the Lord.
But let a man examine himself, and so let him eat of that bread, and drink of that cup.
For he that eateth and drinketh unworthily, eateth and drinketh damnation to himself, not discerning the Lord's body.
For this cause many are weak and sickly among you, and many sleep.
1 Corinthians 11:24-30

CONDEMNATION

Wherefore, as by one man sin entered into the world, and death by sin; and so death passed upon all men, for that all have sinned: Romans 5:12

For God sent not his Son into the world to condemn the world; but that the world through him might be saved.
He that believeth on him is not condemned; but he that believeth not is condemned already, because he hath not believed in the name of the only begotten Son of God.
And this is the condemnation, that light is come into the world, and men loved darkness rather than light, because their deeds were evil. John 3:17-19

There is therefore now no condemnation to them which are in Christ Jesus, who walk not after the flesh, but after the Spirit. Romans 8:1

Therefore thou art inexcusable, O man, whosoever thou art that judgest: for wherein thou judgest another, thou condemnest thyself; for thou that judgest doest the same things. Romans 2:1

For by thy words thou shalt be justified, and by thy words thou shalt be condemned. Matthew 12:37

Beloved, if our heart condemn us not, then have we confidence toward God. 1 John 3:21

CONFESSING CHRIST

Whosoever therefore shall confess me before men, him will I confess also before my Father which is in heaven. Matthew 10:32

That if thou shalt confess with thy mouth the Lord Jesus, and shalt believe in thine heart that God hath raised him from the dead, thou shalt be saved. Romans 10:9

Hereby know ye the Spirit of God: Every spirit that confesseth that Jesus Christ is come in the flesh is of God: 1 John 4:2

Whosoever shall confess that Jesus is the Son of God, God dwelleth in him, and he in God. 1 John 4:15

For many deceivers are entered into the world, who confess not that Jesus Christ is come in the flesh. This is a deceiver and an anti-christ. 2 John 7

CONFESSING SIN

I acknowledged my sin unto thee, and mine iniquity have I not hid. I said, I will confess my transgressions unto the Lord; and thou forgavest the iniquity of my sin. Selah. Psalm 32:5

For I will declare mine iniquity; I will be sorry for my sin. Psalm 38:18

Wash me throughly from mine iniquity, and cleanse me from my sin. For I acknowledge my transgressions: and my sin is ever before me. Against thee, thee only have I sinned, and done this evil in thy sight: that thou mightest be justified when thou speakest, and be clear when thou judgest. Psalm 51:2-4

Hide thy face from my sins, and blot out all mine iniquities. Create in me a clean heart, O God; and renew a right spirit within me. Psalm 51:9-10

He that covereth his sins shall not prosper: but whoso confesseth and forsaketh them shall have mercy. Proverbs 28:13

If we confess our sins, he is faithful and just to forgive us our sins, and to cleanse us from all unrighteousness. 1 John 1:9

CONFORMITY

And be not conformed to this world: but be ye transformed by the renewing of your mind, that ye may prove what is that good, and acceptable, and perfect, will of God. Romans 12:2

As obedient children, not fashioning yourselves according to the former lusts in your ignorance. 1 Peter 1:14

Who shall change our vile body, that it may be fashioned like unto his glorious body, according to the working whereby he is able even to subdue all things unto himself. Philippians 3:21

CORRECTION

I will be his father, and he shall be my son. If he commit iniquity, I will chasten him with the rod of men, and with the stripes of the children of men: 2 Samuel 7:14

He is chastened also with pain upon his bed, and the multitude of his bones with strong pain: Job 33:19

The Lord hath chastened me sore: but he hath not given me over unto death. Psalm 118:18

Judgments are prepared for scorners, and stripes for the back of fools. Proverbs 19:29

Foolishness is bound in the heart of a child; but the rod of correction shall drive it far from him. Proverbs 22:15

Withhold not correction from the child: for if thou beatest him with the rod, he shall not die.
Thou shalt beat him with the rod, and shall deliver his soul from hell. Proverbs 23:13-14

A whip for the horse, a bridle for the donkey, and a rod for the fool's back. Proverbs 26:3 NKJV

And that servant, which knew his lord's will, and prepared not himself, neither did according to his will, shall be beaten with many stripes. Luke 12:47

The rod and reproof give wisdom: but a child left to himself bringeth his mother to shame. Proverbs 29:15

Thou shalt also consider in thine heart, that, as a man chasteneth his son, so the Lord thy God chasteneth thee. Deuteronomy 8:5

Blessed is the man whom thou chastenest, O Lord, and teachest him out of thy law; Psalm 94:12

Now no chastening for the present seemeth to be joyous, but grievous: nevertheless afterward it yieldeth the peaceable fruit of righteousness unto them which are exercised thereby. Hebrews 12:11

Correction is grievous unto him that forsaketh the way: and he that hateth reproof shall die. Proverbs 15:10

O Lord, correct me, but with judgment; not in thine anger, lest thou bring me to nothing. Jeremiah 10:24

My son, despise not the chastening of the Lord; neither be weary of his correction:
For whom the Lord loveth he correcteth; even as a father the son in whom he delighteth. Proverbs 3:11,12

Correct thy son, and he shall give thee rest; yea, he shall give delight unto thy soul. Proverbs 29:17

Behold, happy is the man whom God correcteth: therefore despise not thou the chastening of the Almighty: Job 5:17

All scripture is given by inspiration of God, and is profitable for doctrine, for reproof, for correction, for instruction in righteousness: 2 Timothy 3:16

In the lips of him that hath understanding wisdom is found: but a rod is for the back of him that is void of understanding. Proverbs 10:13

Chasten thy son while there is hope, and let not thy soul spare for his crying. Proverbs 19:18

COUNSEL

Counsel is mine, and sound wisdom: I am understanding; I have strength. Proverbs 8:14

The counsel of the Lord standeth forever, the thoughts of his heart to all generations. Psalm 33:11

With him is wisdom and strength, he hath counsel and understanding. Job 12:13

For unto us a child is born, unto us a son is given: and the government shall be upon his shoulder: and his name shall be called Wonderful, Counsellor, The mighty God, The everlasting Father, The Prince of Peace. Isaiah 9:6

Hear counsel, and receive instruction, that thou mayest be wise in thy latter end. Proverbs 19:20

There are many devices in a man's heart; nevertheless the counsel of the Lord, that shall stand. Proverbs 19:21

Where no counsel is, the people fall: but in the multitude of counsellors there is safety. Proverbs 11:14

Without counsel purposes are disappointed: but in the multitude of counsellors they are established. Proverbs 15:22

Blessed is the man that walketh not in the counsel of the ungodly, nor standeth in the way of sinners, nor sitteth in the seat of the scornful. Psalm 1:1

How long shall I take counsel in my soul, having sorrow in my heart daily? How long shall mine enemy be exalted over me? Psalm 13:2

I will bless the Lord, who hath given me counsel: my reins also instruct me in the night seasons. Psalm 16:7

Counsel in the heart of man is like deep water; but a man of understanding will draw it out. Proverbs 20:5

Thou shalt guide me with thy counsel, and afterward receive me to glory. Psalm 73:24

And they said unto him, Ask counsel, we pray thee, of God, that we may know whether our way which we go shall be prosperous. Judges 18:5

The steps of a good man are ordered by the Lord: and he delighteth in his way. Psalm 37:23

DAMNATION

Woe unto you, scribes and Pharisees, hypocrites! For ye devour widows' houses, and for a pretence make long prayer: therefore ye shall receive the greater damnation. Matthew 23:14

Having damnation, because they have cast off their first faith. 1 Timothy 5:12

DEATH OF A CHRISTIAN

Precious in the sight of the Lord is the death of his saints. Psalm 116:15

The righteous perisheth, and no man layeth it to heart: and merciful men are taken away, none considering that the righteous is taken away from the evil to come.
He shall enter into peace: they shall rest in their beds, each one walking in his uprightness. Isaiah 57:1,2

Henceforth there is laid up for me a crown of righteousness, which the Lord, the righteous judge, shall give me at that day: and not to me only, but unto all them also that love his appearing. 2 Timothy 4:8

For if we believe that Jesus died and rose again, even so them also which sleep in Jesus will God bring with him. 1 Thessalonians 4:14

For to me to live is Christ, and to die is gain. Philippians 1:21

And I heard a voice from heaven saying unto me, Write, Blessed are the dead which die in the Lord from henceforth: Yea, saith the Spirit, that they may rest from their labours; and their works do follow them. Revelation 14:13

We are confident, I say, and willing rather to be absent from the body, and to be present with the Lord. 2 Corinthians 5:8

And they stoned Stephen, calling upon God, and saying, Lord Jesus, receive my spirit.
And he kneeled down, and cried with a load voice, Lord, lay not this sin to their charge. And when he had said this, he fell asleep. Acts 7:59,60

DESIRE

One thing have I desired of the Lord, that will I seek after; that I may dwell in the house of the Lord all the days of my life, to behold the beauty of the Lord, and to enquire in his temple. Psalm 27:4

Delight thyself also in the Lord; and he shall give thee the desires of thine heart. Psalm 37:4

Commit thy way unto the Lord; trust also in him; and he shall bring it to pass. Psalm 37:5

He will fulfil the desire of them that fear him: he also will hear their cry, and will save them. Psalm 145:19

He becometh poor that dealeth with a slack hand: but the hand of the diligent maketh rich. Proverbs 10:4

The fear of the wicked, it shall come upon him: but the desire of the righteous shall be granted. Proverbs 10:24

Through desire a man, having separated himself, seeketh and intermeddleth with all wisdom. Proverbs 18:1

Seest thou a man diligent in his business? He shall stand before kings; he shall not stand before mean men. Proverbs 22:29

But seek ye first the kingdom of God, and his righteousness; and all these things shall be added unto you. Matthew 6:33

This is a true saying, If a man desire the office of a bishop, he desireth a good work. 1 Timothy 3:1

As newborn babes, desire the sincere milk of the word, that ye may grow thereby: 1 Peter 2:2

Follow after charity, and desire spiritual gifts, but rather that ye may prophecy. 1 Corinthians 14:1

Hope deferred maketh the heart sick, but when the desire cometh, it is a tree of life. Proverbs 13:12

The desire of the righteous is only good: but the expectation of the wicked is wrath. Proverbs 11:23

The desire accomplished is sweet to the soul: but it is abomination to fools to depart from evil. Proverbs 13:19

Thou hast given him his heart's desire and hast not withholden the request of his lips. Selah. Psalm 21:2

DISCIPLESHIP

The disciple is not above his master, nor the servant above his lord. Matthew 10:24

Then spake Jesus again unto them, saying, I am the light of the world: he that followeth me shall not walk in darkness, but shall have the light of life. John 8:12

Then said Jesus to those Jews which believed on him, If ye continue in my word, then are ye my disciples indeed; John 8:31

If any man serve me, let him follow me; and where I am, there shall also my servants be: if any man serve me, him will my Father honour: John 12:26

A new commandment I give unto you, That ye love one another; as I have loved you, that ye also love one another.
By this shall all men know that ye are my disciples, if ye have love one to another. John 13:34,35

If ye love me, keep my commandments. John 14:15

Herein is my Father glorified, that ye bear much fruit, so shall ye be my disciples. John 15:8

DIVORCE

But I say unto you, That whosoever shall put away his wife, saving for the cause of fornication, causeth her to commit adultery: and whosoever shall marry her that is divorced committeth adultery. Matthew 5:32

And they said, Moses suffered to write a bill of divorcement, and to put her away.
And Jesus answered and said unto them, For the hardness of your heart he wrote you this precept. Mark10:4,5

What therefore God hath joined together, let no man put asunder. Mark 10:9

For the woman which hath an husband is bound by the law to her husband so long as he liveth; but if the husband be dead, she is loosed from the law of her husband. Romans 7:2

And unto the married I command, yet not I, but the Lord, Let not the wife depart from her husband:

But if she depart, let her remain unmarried, or be reconciled to her husband: and let not the husband put away his wife.

But to the rest speak I, not the Lord: If any brother hath a wife that believeth not, and she be pleased to dwell with him, let him not put her away.

And the woman which hath an husband that believeth not, and if he be pleased to dwell with her, let her not leave him.

For the unbelieving husband is sanctified by the wife, and the unbelieving wife is sanctified by the husband: else were your children unclean; but now are they holy.

But if the unbelieving depart, let him depart. A brother or a sister is not under bondage in such cases: but God hath called us to peace.

For what knowest thou, O wife, whether thou shalt save thy husband? Or how knowest thou, O man, whether thou shalt save thy wife? 1 Corinthians 7:10-16

EDIFICATION

And now, brethren, I commend you to God, and to the word of his grace, which is able to build you up, and to give you an inheritance among all them which are sanctified. Acts 20:32

Let us therefore follow after the things which make for peace, and things wherewith one may edify another. Romans 14:19

Let every one of us please his neighbor for his good to edification. Romans 15:2

Now as touching things offered unto idols, we know that we all have knowledge. Knowledge puffeth up, but charity edifieth. 1 Corinthians 8:1

He that speaketh in an unknown tongue edifieth himself; but he that prophesieth edifieth the church. 1 Corinthians 14:4

And he gave some, apostles; and some, prophets, and some, evangelists; and some, pastors and teachers;
For the perfecting of the saints, for the work of the ministry, for the edifying of the body of Christ. Ephesians 4:11,12

END TIME EVENTS

And this gospel of the kingdom shall be preached in all the world for a witness unto all nations; and then shall the end come. Matthew 24:14

Knowing this first, that there shall come in the last days scoffers, walking after there own lusts,
And saying, Where is the promise of his coming? For since the fathers fell asleep, all things continue as they were from the beginning of the creation. 2 Peter 3:3,4

The Son of man shall send forth his angels, and they shall gather out of his kingdom all things that offend, and them which do iniquity;
And shall cast them into a furnace of fire: there shall be wailing and gnashing of teeth.
Then shall the righteous shine forth as the sun in the kingdom of their Father. Who hath ears to hear, let him hear. Matthew 13:41-43

For many shall come in my name, saying, I am Christ; and shall deceive many.
And ye shall hear of wars and rumours of wars: see that ye be not troubled: for all these things must come to pass, but the end is not yet.
For nation shall rise against nation, and kingdom against kingdom: and there shall be famines, and pestilences, and earthquakes, in divers places.
All these are the beginning of sorrows. Matthew 24:5-8

And many false prophets shall rise, and shall deceive many.
And because iniquity shall abound, the love of many shall wax cold.

But he that shall endure unto the end, the same shall be saved. Matthew 24:11,13

Let no man deceive you by any means: for that day shall not come, except there come a falling away first, and that man of sin be revealed, the son of perdition;
Who opposeth and exalteth himself above all that is called God, or that is worshipped; so that he as God sitteth in the temple of God, shewing himself that he is God. 2 Thessalonians 2:3,4

And then shall that Wicked be revealed, whom the Lord shall consume with the spirit of his mouth, and shall destroy with the brightness of his coming:
Even him, whose coming is after the working of Satan with all power and signs and lying wonders,
And with all deceivableness of unrighteousness in them that perish; because they received not the love of truth, that they might be saved.
And for this cause God shall send them strong delusion, that they should believe a lie:
That they all might be damned who believed not the truth, but had pleasure in unrighteousness. 2 Thessalonians 2:8-12

This know also, that in the last days perilous times shall come.
For men shall be lovers of their own selves, covetous, boasters, proud, blasphemers, disobedient to parents, unthankful, unholy
Without natural affection, trucebreakers, false accusers, incontinent, fierce despisers of those that are good,
Traitors, heady, highminded, lovers of pleasures more than lovers of God;
Having a form of godliness, but denying the power thereof: from such turn away.
For of this sort are they which creep into houses, and lead captive silly women laden with sins, led away with divers lusts,

Ever learning, and never able to come to the knowledge of the truth. 2 Timothy 3:1-7

Yea, and all that will live godly in Christ Jesus shall suffer persecution. But evil men and seducers shall wax worse and worse, deceiving and being deceived. 2 Timothy 3:12,13

ENDURANCE

And ye shall be hated of all men for my name's sake: but he that endureth to the end shall be saved. Matthew 10:22

Heaven and earth shall pass away, but my words shall not pass away. Matthew 24:35

Labour not for the meat which perisheth, but for that meat which endureth unto everlasting life, which the Son of man shall give unto you: for him hath God the Father sealed. John 6:27

Thou therefore endure hardness, as a good soldier of Jesus Christ. 2 Timothy 2:3

Therefore I endure all things for the elect's sakes, that they may also obtain the salvation which is in Christ Jesus with eternal glory. 2 Timothy 2:10

Persecutions, afflictions, which came unto me at Antioch, at Iconium, at Lystra; what persecutions I endured; but out of them all the Lord delivered me. 2 Timothy 3:11

ETERNAL LIFE

And every one that hath forsaken houses, or brethren, or sisters, or father, or mother, or wife, or children, or lands, for my name's sake, shall receive an hundred-fold, and shall inherit everlasting life. Matthew 19:29

That whosoever believeth in him should not perish, but have eternal life. John 3:15

But whosoever drinketh of the water that I shall give him shall never thirst; but the water that I shall give him shall be in him a well of water springing up into everlasting life. John 4:14

Verily, verily, I say unto you, He that heareth my word, and believeth on him that sent me, hath everlasting life, and shall not come into condemnation: but is passed from death unto life. John 5:24

And Jesus said unto them, I am the bread of life: he that cometh to me shall never hunger; and he that believeth on me shall never thirst. John 6:35

Then Simon Peter answered him, Lord, to whom shall we go? Thou hast the words of eternal life. John 6:68

My sheep hear my voice, and I know them, and they follow me:
And I give unto them eternal life; and they shall never perish, neither shall any man pluck them out of my hand. John 10:27,28

As thou hast given him power over all flesh, that he should give eternal life to as many as thou hast given him.
And this is life eternal, that they might know thee the only true God, and Jesus Christ, whom thou hast sent. John 17:2,3

But these are written, that ye might believe that Jesus is the Christ, the Son of God; and that believing ye might have life through his name. John 20:31

That as sin hath reigned unto death, even so might grace reign through righteousness unto eternal life by Jesus Christ our Lord. Romans 5:21

But now being made free from sin, and become servants to God, ye have your fruit unto holiness, and the end everlasting life. Romans 6:22

For the wages of sin is death; but the gift of God is eternal life through Jesus Christ our Lord. Romans 6:23

For he that soweth to his flesh shall of the flesh reap corruption: but he that soweth to the Spirit shall of the Spirit reap life everlasting. Galatians 6:8

Fight the good fight of faith, lay hold on eternal life, whereunto thou art also called, and hast professed a good profession before many witnesses. 1 Timothy 6:12

Laying up in store for themselves a good foundation against the time to come, that they may lay hold on eternal life. 1 Timothy 6:19

In hope of eternal life, which God, that cannot lie, promised before the world began; Titus 1:2

And this is the record, that God hath given to us eternal life, and this life is in his Son.1 John 5:11

FAITH IN GOD

Now faith is the substance of things hoped for, the evidence of things not seen. Hebrews 11:1

And Caleb stilled the people before Moses, and said, Let us go up at once, and possess it; for we are well able to overcome it. Numbers 13:30

Behold, his soul which is lifted up is not upright in him: but the just shall live by his faith. Habakkuk 2:4

And all things, whatsoever ye shall ask in prayer, believing, ye shall receive. Matthew 21:22

He that believeth and is baptized shall be saved; but he that believeth not shall be damned.
And these signs shall follow them that believe; In my name shall they cast out devils; they shall speak with new tongues;
They shall take up serpents; and if they drink any deadly thing, it shall not hurt them; they shall lay hands on the sick, and they shall recover. Mark 16:16-18

For she said, If I may touch his clothes, I shall be whole. Mark 5:28

But as many as received him, to them gave he power to become the sons of God, even to them that believe on his name: John 1:12

That whosoever believeth in him should not perish, but have eternal life. John 3:15

While ye have light, believe in the light, that ye may be the children of light…John 12:36

I am come a light into the world, that whosoever believeth on me should not abide in darkness. John 12:46

Confirming the souls of the disciples, and exhorting them to continue in the faith, and that we must through much tribulation enter into the kingdom of God. Acts 14:22

To him give all the prophets witness, that through his name whosoever believeth in him shall receive remission of sins. Acts 10:43

And being fully persuaded that, what he had promised, he was able also to perform. Romans 4:21

Therefore being justified by faith, we have peace with God through our Lord Jesus Christ: Romans 5:1

Watch ye, stand fast in the faith, quit you like men, be strong. 1 Corinthians 16:13

For by grace are ye saved through faith; and that not of yourselves: it is the gift of God: Ephesians 2:8

In whom we have boldness and access with confidence by the faith of him. Ephesians 3:12

Above all, taking the shield of faith, wherewith ye shall be able to quench all the fiery darts of the wicked. Ephesians 6:16

Fight the good fight of faith, lay hold on eternal life, whereunto thou art also called, and hast professed a good profession before many witnesses. 1 Timothy 6:12

Let us hold fast the profession of our faith without wavering; (for he is faithful that promised;) Hebrews 10:23

Let us draw near with a true heart in full assurance of faith, having our hearts sprinkled from an evil conscience, and our bodies washed with pure water. Hebrews 10:22

But without faith it is impossible to please him: for he that cometh to God must believe that he is, and that he is a rewarder of them that diligently seek him. Hebrews 11:6

Even so faith, if it hath not works, is dead, being alone. James 2:17

But wilt thou know, O vain man, that faith without works is dead? James 2:20

And the prayer of faith shall save the sick, and the Lord shall raise him up; and if he have committed sins, they shall be forgiven him. James 5:15

That the trial of your faith, being much more precious than of gold that perisheth, though it be tried with fire, might be found unto praise and honour and glory at the appearing of Jesus Christ: 1 Peter 1:7

(For we walk by faith, not by sight:) 2 Corinthians 5:7

So then faith cometh by hearing, and hearing by the word of God. Romans 10:17

But that no man is justified by the law in the sight of God, it is evident: for, The just shall live by faith. Galatians 3:11

That your faith should not stand in the wisdom of men, but in the power of God. 1 Corinthians 2:5

FASTING

And Jesus said unto them, Can the children of the bridechamber mourn, as long as the bridegroom is with them? But the days will come, when the bridegroom shall be taken from them, and then shall they fast. Matthew 9:15

Moreover when you fast, be not, as the hypocrites, of a sad countenance: for they disfigure their faces, that they may appear unto men to fast. Verily I say unto you, They have their reward.
But thou, when thou fastest, anoint thine head, and wash thy face;
That thou appear not unto men to fast, but unto thy Father which is in secret: and thy Father which seeth in secret, shall reward thee openly. Matthew 6:16-18

But as for me, when they were sick, my clothing was sackcloth: I humbled my soul with fasting; and my prayer returned into mine own bosom. Psalm 35:13

When I wept, and chastened my soul with fasting, that was to my reproach. Psalm 69:10

Defraud ye not one the other, except it be with consent for a time, that ye may give yourselves to fasting and prayer; and come together again, that Satan tempt you not for your incontinency. 1 Corinthians 7:5

FAVOR

For they got not the land in possession by their own sword, neither did their own arm save them: but thy right hand, and thine arm, and the light of thy countenance, because thou hadst a favour unto them. Psalm 44:3

For whoso findeth me findeth life, and shall obtain favour of the Lord. Proverbs 8:35

Get wisdom, get understanding: forget it not; neither decline from the words of my mouth.
Forsake her not, and she shall preserve thee: love her, and she shall keep thee. Proverbs 4:5,6

Whoso findeth a wife findeth a good thing, and obtaineth favour of the Lord. Proverbs 18:22

Then this Daniel was preferred above the presidents and princes because an excellent spirit was in him; and the king thought to set him over the whole realm. Daniel 6:3

And in the sixth month the angel Gabriel was sent from God unto a city of Galilee, named Nazareth,
To a virgin espoused to a man whose name was Joseph, of the house of David; and the virgin's name was Mary.
And the angel came in unto her, and said, Hail, thou that art highly

favoured, the Lord is with thee: blessed art thou among women. Luke 1:26-28

The king's favour is toward a wise servant; but his wrath is against him that causeth shame. Proverbs 14:35

When a man's ways please the Lord, he maketh even his enemies to be at peace with him. Proverbs 16:7

In the light of the king's countenance is life; and his favour is as a cloud of the latter rain. Proverbs 16:15

The king's wrath is as the roaring of a lion; but his favour is as due upon the grass. Proverbs 19:12

And it was so, when the king saw Ester the queen standing in the court, that she obtained favour in his sight:... Ester 5:2

For thou, Lord, wilt bless the righteous: with favour wilt thou compass him as with a shield. Psalm 5:12

So shalt thou find favour and good understanding in the sight of God and man. Proverbs 3:4

And the Lord gave the people favour in the sight of the Egyptians, so that they lent unto them such things as they required. And they spoiled the Egyptians. Exodus 12:36

Then Peter opened his mouth, and said, Of a truth I perceive that God is no respecter of persons: Acts 10:34

FEAR

For God hath not given us the spirit of fear, but of power, and of love, and of a sound mind. 2 Timothy 1:7

Yea, though I walk through the valley of the shadow of death, I will fear no evil; for thou art with me; thy rod and thy staff they comfort me. Psalm 23:4

The Lord is my light and my salvation; whom shall I fear? The Lord is the strength of my life, of whom shall I be afraid. Psalm 27:1

In God have I put my trust, I will not be afraid what man can do unto me. Psalm 56:11

And fear not them which kill the body, but are not able to kill the soul: but rather fear him which is able to destroy both soul and body in hell. Matthew 10:28

There is no fear in love; but perfect love casteth out fear: because fear hath torment. He that feareth is not made perfect in love. 1 John 4:18

FELLOWSHIP

And the Lord said, Behold, the people is one, and they have all one language, and this they begin to do; and now nothing will be restrained from them, which they have imagined to do. Gen 11:6

Praise ye the Lord, I will praise the Lord with my whole heart, in the assembly of the upright, and in the congregation. Psalm 111:1

Behold, how good and how pleasant it is for brethren to dwell together in unity! Psalm 133:1

Can two walk together, except they be agreed? Amos 3:3

These all continued with one accord in prayer and supplication, with the women, and Mary the mother of Jesus, and with his brethren. Acts 1:14

And they continued stedfastly in the apostles' doctrine and fellowship, and in breaking of bread, and in prayers. Acts 2:42

And all that believed were together, and had all things common; Acts 2:44

And they, continuing daily with one accord in the temple, and breaking bread from house to house, did eat their meat with gladness and singleness of heart, Acts 2:46

And when they had prayed, the place was shaken where they were assembled together; and they were all filled with the Holy Ghost, and they spake the word of God with boldness. Acts 4:31

And the people with one accord gave heed unto those things which Philip spake, hearing and seeing the miracles which he did. Acts 8:6

It seemed good unto us, being assembled with one accord, to send chosen men unto you with our beloved Barnabas and Paul, Acts 15:25

Be of the same mind one toward another. Mind not high things, but condescend to men of low estate. Be not wise in your own conceits. Romans 12:16

God is faithful, by whom ye were called unto the fellowship of his Son Jesus Christ our Lord. 1 Corinthians 1:9

Ye cannot drink the cup of the Lord, and the cup of devils: ye cannot be partakers of the Lord's table, and of the table of devils. 1 Corinthians 10:21

And have no fellowship with the unfruitful works of darkness, but rather reprove them. Ephesians 5:11

If there be therefore any consolation in Christ, if any comfort of love, if any fellowship of the Spirit, if any bowels and mercies.

Fulfil ye my joy, that ye be likeminded, having the same love, being of one accord, of one mind.
Let nothing be done through strive or vainglory; but in lowliness of mind let each esteem other better than themselves.
Look not every man on his own things, but every man also on the things of others. Philippians 2:1-4

That I may know him, and the power of his resurrection, and the fellowship of his sufferings, being made conformable unto his death; Philippians 3:10

Not forsaking the assembling of ourselves together, as the manner of some is; but exhorting one another: and so much the more, as ye see the day approaching. Hebrews 10:25

Finally, be ye all of one mind, having compassion one of another, love as brethren, be pitiful, be courteous: 1 Peter 3:8

That which we have seen and heard declare we unto you, that ye also may have fellowship with us: and truly our fellowship is with the Father, and with his Son Jesus Christ. 1 John 1:3

If we say that we have fellowship with him, and walk in darkness, we lie, and do not the truth:
But if we walk in the light, as he is in the light, we have fellowship one with another, and the blood of Jesus Christ his Son cleanseth us from all sin. 1 John 1:6,7

Be ye not unequally yoked together with unbelievers: for what fellowship hath righteousness with unrighteousness? And what communion hath light with darkness? 2 Corinthians 6:14

Now I beseech you, brethren, by the name of our Lord Jesus Christ, that ye all speak the same thing, and that there be no divisions among you; but that ye be perfectly joined together in the same mind and in the same judgment. 1 Corinthians 1:10

Be not deceived: evil communications corrupt good manners. 1 Corinthians 15:33

FIRSTFRUITS

And Abel, he also brought of the firstlings of his flock and of the fat thereof. And the Lord had respect unto Abel and to his offering: Genesis 4:4

The first of the firstfruits of thy land thou shalt bring unto the house of the Lord thy God.
Thou shalt not seethe a kid in his mother's milk. Exodus 34:26

Speak unto the children of Israel, and say unto them, When ye be come into the land which I give unto you, and shall reap the harvest thereof, then ye shall bring a sheaf of the firstfruits of your harvest unto the priest. Leviticus 23:10

And ye shall eat neither bread, nor parched corn, nor green ears, until the selfsame day that ye have brought an offering unto your God: it shall be a statue for ever throughout your generations in all your dwellings. Leviticus 23:14

That thou shalt take of the first of all the fruit of the earth, which thou shalt bring of thy land that the Lord thy God giveth thee, and shalt put it in a basket, and shalt go unto the place which the Lord thy God shall choose to place his name there. Deuteronomy 26:2

And as soon as the commandment came abroad, the children of Israel brought in abundance the firstfruit of corn, wine, and oil, and honey, and of all the increase of the field; and the tithe of all things brought they in abundantly. 2 Chronicles 31:5

And Azariah the chief priest of the house of Zadok answered him, and said, Since the people began to bring the offerings into the house of the

Lord, we have had enough to eat, and have left plenty: for the Lord hath blessed his people; and that which is left is this great store. 2 Chronicles 31:10

Honour the Lord with thy substance, and with the firstfruits of all thine increase:
So shall thy barns be filled with plenty, and thy presses shall burst out with new wine. Proverbs 3:9,10

And the first of all the firstfruits of all things, and every oblation of all, of every sort of your oblations, shall be the priest's: ye shall also give unto the priest the first of your dough, that he may cause the blessing to rest in thine house. Ezekiel 44:30

And they shall not sell of it, neither exchange, nor alienate the first-fruits of the land: for it is holy unto the Lord. Ezekiel 48:14

For if the firstfruit be holy, the lump is also holy: and if the root be holy, so are the branches. Romans 11:16

But now is Christ risen from the dead, and become the firstfruits of them that slept. 1 Corinthians 15:20

Of his own will begat he us with the word of truth, that we should be a kind of firstfruits of his creatures. James 1:18

FORGIVENESS

For thou, Lord, art good, and ready to forgive; and plenteous in mercy unto all them that call upon thee. Psalm 86:5

I, even I, am he that blotted out thy transgressions, for mine own sake, and will not remember thy sins. Isaiah 43:25

Let the wicked forsake his way, and the unrighteous man his thoughts: and let him return unto the Lord, and he will have mercy upon him; and to our God, for he will abundantly pardon. Isaiah 55:7

And they shall teach no more every man his neighbor, and every man his brother, saying, Know the Lord: for they shall all know me, from the least of them unto the greatest of them, saith the Lord: for I will forgive their iniquity, and I will remember their sin no more. Jeremiah 31:34

And forgive us our debts, as we forgive our debtors. Matthew 6:12

For if ye forgive men their trespasses, your heavenly Father will also forgive you:
But if ye forgive not men their trespasses, neither will your Father forgive your trespasses. Matthew 6:14,15

Wherefore I say unto you, All manner of sin and blasphemy shall be forgiven unto men: but the blasphemy against the Holy Ghost shall not be forgiven unto men. Matthew 12:31

Then came Peter to him, and said, Lord, how oft shall my brother sin against me, and I forgive him? Till seven times?
Jesus said unto him, I say not unto thee, Until seven times: but, Until seventy times seven. Matthew 18:21,22

For this is my blood of the new testament, which is shed for many for the remission of sins. Matthew 26:28

And when ye stand praying, forgive, if ye have ought against any: that your Father also which is in heaven may forgive you your trespasses. Mark 11:25

Take heed to yourselves: If thy brethren trespass against thee, rebuke him; and if he repent, forgive him.
And if he trespass against thee seven times in a day, and seven times in

a day turn again to thee, saying, I repent; thou shalt forgive him. Luke 17:3,4

To him give all the prophets witness, that through his name whosoever believeth in him shall receive remission of sins. Acts 10:43

And be ye kind one to another, tenderhearted, forgiving one another, even as God for Christ's sake hath forgiven you. Ephesians 4:32

In whom we have redemption through his blood, even the forgiveness of sins: Colossians 1:14

Forbearing one another, and forgiving one another, if any man have a quarrel against any: even as Christ forgave you, so also do ye. Colossians 3:13

FORNICATION

I wrote unto you in an epistle not to company with fornicators: 1 Corinthians 5:9

But now I have written unto you not to keep company, if any man that is called a brother be a fornicator, or covetous, or an idolater, or a railor, or a drunkard, or an extortioner, with such an one no not to eat. 1 Corinthians 5:11

Know ye not that the unrighteous shall not inherit the kingdom of God? Be not deceived: neither fornicators, nor idolaters, nor adulterers, nor effeminate, or abusers of themselves with mankind,
Nor thieves, nor covetous, nor drunkards, nor revilers, nor extortioners, shall inherit the kingdom of God. 1 Corinthians 6:9,10

Meats for the belly, and the belly for meats: but God shall destroy both it and them. Now the body is not for fornication, but for the Lord; and the Lord for the body. 1 Corinthians 6:13

Flee fornication, Every sin that a man doeth is without the body; but he that committeth fornication sinneth against his own body.

What? Know ye not that your body is the temple of the Holy Ghost which is in you, which ye have of God, and ye are not your own? 1 Corinthians 6:18,19

FRUIT OF THE WOMB

Jesus said unto him, If thou canst believe, all things are possible to him that believeth. Mark 9:23

And God blessed them, and God said unto them, Be fruitful, and multiply, and replenish the earth, and subdue it… Gen 1:28

Blessed shall be the fruit of thy body… Deuteronomy 28:4

And the Lord shall make thee plenteous in goods, in the fruit of the body…Deuteronomy 28:11

So Boaz took Ruth, and she was his wife: and when he went in unto her, the Lord gave her conception, and she bare a son. Ruth 4:13

And she vowed a vow, and said, O Lord of hosts, if thou wilt indeed look on the affliction of thine handmaid, and remember me, and not forget thine handmaid, but wilt give unto thine handmaid a man child, then I will give him unto the Lord all the days of his life… 1 Samuel 1:11

...Elkanah knew Hannah his wife; and the Lord remembered her. Wherefore it can to pass, when the time was come about after Hannah had conceived, that she bare a son, and called his name Samuel, saying, Because I have asked him of the Lord. 1 Samuel 1:19,20

For this child I prayed; and the Lord hath given me my petition which I asked of Him. 1 Samuel 1:27

...Thus saith the Lord, I have healed these waters; there shall not be from thence any more death or barren land. 2 Kings 2:21

Lo, children are an heritage of the Lord: and the fruit of the womb is his reward. Psalm 127:3

Thy wife shall be as a fruitful vine by the sides of thine house: thy children like olive plants round about thy table. Psalm 128:3

He maketh a barren woman to keep house, and to be a joyful mother of children. Praise ye the Lord. Psalm 113:9

I will praise thee; for I am fearfully and wonderfully made: marvelous are thy works; and that my soul knoweth right well. Psalm 139:14

Before I formed thee in the belly I knew thee; and before thou camest forth out of the womb I sanctified thee, and ordained thee a prophet unto the nations. Jeremiah 1:5

But when it pleased God, who separated me from my mother's womb, and called me by his grace, Galatians 1:15

GOODNESS OF GOD

And the Lord passed by before him, and proclaimed, The Lord, the Lord God, merciful and gracious, longsuffering, and abundant in goodness and truth, Exodus 34:6

Oh how great is thy goodness, which thou hast laid up for them that fear thee; which thou hast wrought for them that trust in thee before the sons of men! Psalm 31:19

Blessed is the man whom thou choosest, and causest to approach unto thee, that he may dwell in thy courts: we shall be satisfied with the goodness of thy house, even of thy holy temple. Psalm 65:4

Thou hast caused men to ride over our heads; we went through fire and through water: but thou broughtest us out into a wealthy place. Psalm 66:12

For thou, Lord, art good, and ready to forgive; and plenteous in mercy unto all them that call upon thee. Psalm 86:5

The Lord is gracious, and full of compassion; slow to anger, and of great mercy.
The Lord is good to all: and his tender mercies are over all his works. Psalm 145:8,9

GOSSIP

Thou shalt not go up and down as a talebearer among thy people: neither shalt thou stand against the blood of thy neighbor: I am the Lord. Leviticus 19:16

A talebearer revealeth secrets: but he that is of a faithful spirit concealeth the matter. Proverbs 11:13

A froward man soweth strife: and a whisperer seperateth chief friends. Proverbs 16:28

He that goeth about as a talebearer revealeth secrets: therefore meddle not with him that flattereth with his lips. Proverbs 20:19

HALLOWEEN

Beloved, do not imitate what is evil, but what is good. He who does good is of God, but he who does evil has not seen God. 3 John 11 NKJV

All things are lawful for me, but not all things are helpful; all things are lawful for me, but not all things edify. 1 Corinthians 10:23 NKJV

One man esteemeth one day above another: another esteemeth every day alike. Let every man be fully persuaded in his own mind. Romans 14:5

Let love, be without hypocrisy. Abhor what is evil. Cling to what is good. Romans 12:9 NKJV

Do not be unequally yoked together with unbelievers. For what fellowship has righteousness with lawlessness? And what communion has light with darkness? 2 Corinthians 6:14 NKJV

For you were once darkness, but now you are light in the Lord. Walk as children of light
(for the fruit of the Spirit is in all goodness, righteousness and truth), finding out what is acceptable to the Lord.
And have no fellowship with the unfruitful works of darkness, but rather expose them. Ephesians 5:8-11 NKJV

Abstain from every form of evil. 1 Thessalonians 5:22 NKJV

But I say, that the things which the Gentiles sacrifice, they sacrifice to devils, and not to God: and I would not that ye have fellowship with devils.
Ye cannot drink the cup of the Lord, and the cup of devils: ye cannot be partakers of the Lord's table, and of the table of devils. 1 Corinthians 10:20,21

Thou shalt not suffer a witch to live. Exodus 22:18

In whom the god of this world hath blinded the minds of them which believe not, less the light of the glorious gospel of Christ, who is the image of God, should shine unto them. 2 Corinthians 4:4

Regard not them that have familiar spirits, neither seek after wizards, to be defiled by them: I am the Lord your God. Leviticus 19:31

And when thou art come into the land which the Lord thy God giveth thee, thou shalt not learn to do after the abominations of those nations. There shall not be found among you any one that maketh his son or his daughter to pass through fire, or that useth divination, or an observer of times, or an enchanter, or a witch,
Or an charmer, or a consulter with familiar spirits, or a wizard, or a necromancer. Deuteronomy 18:9-11

And no marvel, for Satan himself is transformed into an angel of light. Therefore it is no great thing if his ministers also be transformed as the ministers of righteousness; whose end shall be according to their works. 2 Corinthians 11:14,15

The earth also was corrupt before God, and the earth was filled with violence. Genesis 6:11

Thou shalt not raise a false report: put not thine hand with the wicked to be an unrighteous witness.
Thou shalt not follow a multitude to do evil; neither shalt thou speak in a cause to decline after many to wrest judgment: Exodus 23:1,2

The Lord trieth the righteous: but the wicked and him that loveth violence his soul hateth. Psalm 11:5

Be not thou envious of evil men, neither desire to be with them. Proverbs 24:1

HEALING

So Abraham prayed unto God: and God healed Abimelech, and his wife, and his maidservants; and they bare children. Genesis 20:17

If my people, which are called by my name, shall humble themselves, and pray, and seek my face, and turn from their wicked ways; then will I hear from heaven, and will forgive their sin, and will heal their land. 2 Chronicles 7:14

Bless the Lord, O my soul, and forget not all his benefits:
Who forgiveth all thine iniquities; who healeth all thy diseases; Psalm 103:2,3

He sent his word, and healed them, and delivered them from their destructions. Psalm 107:20

He healeth the broken in heart, and bindeth up their wounds. Psalm 147:3

And the king answered and said unto the man of God, Intreat now the face of the Lord thy God, and pray for me, that my hand may be restored me again. And the man of God besought the Lord, and the king's hand was restored him again, and became as it was before. 1 Kings 13:6

But he was wounded for our transgressions, he was bruised for our iniquities: the chastisement of our peace was upon him; and with his stripes we are healed. Isaiah 53:5

Heal me, O Lord, and I shall be healed; save me, and I shall be saved: for thou art my praise. Jeremiah 17:14

Return, ye backsliding children, and I will heal your backslidings. Behold, we come unto thee; for thou art the Lord our God. Jeremiah 3:22

But unto you that fear my name shall the Sun of righteousness arise with healing in his wings; and ye shall go forth, and grow up as calves of the stall. Malachi 4:2

When the even was come, they brought unto him many that were possessed with devils: and he cast out the spirits with his word, and healed all that were sick. Matthew 8:16

And when he had called unto him his twelve disciples, and he gave them power against unclean spirits, to cast them out, and to heal all manner of sickness and all manner of disease. Matthew 10:1

And as ye go, preach, saying, The kingdom of heaven is at hand. Heal the sick, cleanse the lepers, raise the dead, cast out devils: freely ye have received, freely give. Matthew 10:7,8

Jesus saith unto him, Go thy way; thy son liveth. And the man believed the word that Jesus had spoken unto him, and he went his way. And as he was now going down, his servants met him, and told him, saying, Thy son liveth. John 4:50,51

Now there are diversities of gifts, but the same Spirit. 1 Corinthians 12:4
To another faith by the same Spirit; to another the gifts of healing by the same Spirit; 1 Corinthians 12:9

And the prayer of faith shall save the sick, and the Lord shall raise him up; and if he have committed sins, they shall be forgiven him. Confess your faults one to another, and pray one for another, that ye may be healed. The effectual fervent prayer of a righteous man availeth much. James 5:15,16

Who his own self bare our sins in his own body on the tree, that we, being dead to sins, should live unto righteousness: by whose stripes ye were healed. 1 Peter 2:24

And he shewed me a pure river of water of life, clear as crystal, proceeding out of the throne of God and of the Lamb.
In the midst of the street of it, and on either side of the river, was there the tree of life, which bare twelve manner of fruits, and yielded her fruit every month: and the leaves of the tree were for the healing of the nations. Revelation 22:1,2

HEAVEN

Blessed are the poor in spirit: for their's is the kingdom of heaven. Matthew 5:3

Blessed are they which are persecuted for righteousness' sake: for their's is the kingdom of heaven. Matthew 5:10

Notwithstanding in this rejoice not, that the spirits are subject unto you; but rather rejoice, because your names are written in heaven. Luke 10:20

I say unto you, that likewise joy shall be in heaven over one sinner that repenteth, more than over ninety and nine just persons, which need no repentance. Luke 15:7

And it came to pass, that the beggar died, and was carried by the angels into Abraham's bosom: the rich man also died, and was buried; Luke 16:22

Likewise, I say unto you, there is joy in the presence of the angels of God over one sinner that repenteth. Luke 15:10

Jesus answered, Verily, verily, I say unto thee, Except a man be born of water and of the Spirit, he cannot enter into the kingdom of God. John 3:5

In my Father's house are many mansions: if it were not so, I would have told you. I go to prepare a place for you.

And if I go and prepare a place for you, I will come again, and receive you unto myself; that where I am, there ye may be also. John 14:2,3

Be he, (Stephen) being full of the Holy Ghost, looked up steadfastly into heaven, and saw the glory of God, and Jesus standing on the right hand of God, Acts 7:55

For he looked for a city which hath foundations, whose builder and maker is God. Hebrews 11:10

But ye are come unto mount Sion, and unto the city of the living God, the heavenly Jerusalem, and to an innumerable company of angels, Hebrews 12:22

Nevertheless we, according to his promise, look for new heavens and a new earth, wherein dwelleth righteousness. 2 Peter 3:13

He that hath an ear, let him hear what the Spirit saith unto the churches; To him that overcometh will I give to eat of the tree of life, which is in the midst of the paradise of God. Revelation 2:7

He that hath an ear, let him hear what the Spirit saith unto the churches; He that overcometh shall not be hurt of the second death. Revelation 2:11

For the Lamb which is in the midst of the throne shall feed them, and shall lead them unto living fountains of waters: and God shall wipe away all tears from their eyes. Revelation 7:17

And God shall wipe away all tears from their eyes; and there shall be no more death, neither sorrow, nor crying, neither shall there be any more pain: for the former things are passed away. Revelation 21:4

HELL

And whosoever shall not receive you, nor hear your words, when ye depart out of that house or city, shake off the dust of your feet.
Verily I say unto you, It shall be more tolerable for the land of Sodom and Gomorrha in the day of judgment, than for that city. Matthew 10:14,15

And before him shall be gathered all nations: and he shall separate them one from another, as a shepherd divideth his sheep from the goats: Matthew 25:32
Then shall he say unto them on the left hand, Depart from me, ye cursed, into everlasting fire, prepared for the devil and his angels: Matthew 25:41
And these shall go away into everlasting punishment: but the righteous into life eternal.
Matthew 25:46

...the rich man also died, and was buried;
And in hell he lifted up his eyes, being in torments, and seeth Abraham afar off, and Lazarus in his bosom. Luke 16:22,23

In flaming fire taking vengeance on them that know not God, and that obey not the gospel of our Lord Jesus Christ.
Who shall be punished with everlasting destruction from the presence of the Lord, and from the glory of his power; 2 Thessalonians 1:8,9

For if God spared not the angels that sinned, but cast them down to hell, and delivered them into chains of darkness, to be reserved unto judgment; 2 Peter 2:4

The Lord knoweth how to deliver the godly out of temptations, and to reserve the unjust unto the day of judgment to be punished: 2 Peter 2:9

And the smoke of their torment ascendeth up for ever and ever; and they have no rest day nor night, who worship the beast and his image, and whosoever receiveth the mark of his name. Revelation 14:11

And the beast was taken, and with him the false prophet that wrought miracles before him, with which he deceived them that had received the mark of the beast, and them that worshipped his image. These both were cast alive into a lake of fire burning with brimstone. Revelation 19:20

And the devil that deceived them was cast into the lake of fire and brimstone, where the beast and the false prophet are, and shall be tormented day and night for ever and ever. Revelation 20:10

And death and hell were cast into the lake of fire. This is the second death.
And whosoever was not found written in the book of life was cast into the lake of fire. Revelation 20:14,15

But the fearful, and unbelieving, and the abominable, and murderers, and whoremongers,and sorcerers, and idolaters, and all liars, shall have their part in the lake which burneth with fire and brimstone: which is the second death. Revelation 21:8

THE HOLY SPIRIT

And the Lord said, My spirit shall not always strive with man, for that he also is flesh: yet his days shall be an hundred and twenty years. Genesis 6:3

The Spirit of God hath made me, and the breath of the Almighty God hath given me life. Job 33:4

Curse not the king, no not in thy thought; and curse not the rich in thy bedchamber: for a bird of the air shall carry the voice, and that which hath wings shall tell the matter. Ecclesiastes 10:20

Jesus answered, Verily, verily, I say unto thee, Except a man be born of water and of the Spirit, he cannot enter into the kingdom of God. John 3:5

And I will pray the Father, and he shall give you another Comforter, that he may abide with you forever;
Even the Spirit of truth, whom the world cannot receive, because it seeth him not, neither knoweth him: but ye know him; for he dwelleth with you, and shall be in you. John 14:16,17

But the Comforter, which is the Holy Ghost, whom the Father will send in my name, he shall teach you all things, and bring all things to your rememberance, whatsoever I have said unto you. John 14:26

And when he is come, he will reprove the world of sin, and of righteousness, and of judgment: John 16:8

Howbeit when he, the Spirit of truth, is come, he will guide you into all truth: for he shall not speak of himself; but whatsoever he shall hear, that shall he speak: and he will shew you things to come. John 16:13

Men and brethren, this scripture must needs have been fulfilled, which the Holy Ghost by the mouth of David spake before concerning Judas, which was guide to them that took Jesus. Acts 1:16

And it shall come to pass in the last days, saith God, I will pour out my Spirit upon all flesh: and your sons and your daughters shall prophecy, and your young men shall see visions, and your old men shall dream dreams: Acts 2:17

Ye stiffnecked and uncircumcised in heart and ears, ye do always resist the Holy Ghost: as your fathers did, so do ye. Acts 7:51

Then had the churches rest throughout all Judea and Galilee and Samaria, and were edified; and walking in the fear of the Lord, and in the comfort of the Holy Ghost, were multiplied. Acts 9:31

But if the Spirit of him that raised up Jesus from the dead dwell in you, he that raised up Christ from the dead shall also quicken your mortal bodies by his Spirit that dwelleth in you. Romans 8:11

Likewise the Spirit also helpeth our infirmities: for we know not what we should pray for as we ought: but the Spirit itself maketh intercession for us with groanings which cannot be uttered. Romans 8:26

For as many as are led by the Spirit of God, they are the sons of God. Romans 8:14

The Spirit itself beareth witness with our spirit, that we are the children of God. Romans 8:16

For the kingdom of God is not meat and drink; but righteousness, and peace, and joy in the Holy Ghost. Romans 14:17

But as it is written, Eye hath not seen, nor ear heard, neither have entered into the heart of man, the things which God hath prepared for them that love him.
But God hath revealed them to us by his Spirit: for the Spirit searcheth all things, yea, the deep things of God. 1 Corinthians 2:9,10

Wherefore I give you to understand, that no man speaking by the Spirit of God calleth Jesus accursed: and that no man can say that Jesus is the Lord, but by the Holy Ghost. 1 Corinthians 12:3

Now there are diversities of gifts, but the same Spirit. 1 Corinthians 12:4

But the manifestation of the Spirit is given to every man to profit withal. 1 Corinthians 12:7

(For the fruit of the Spirit is in all goodness and righteousness and truth;) Ephesians 5:9

But the fruit of the Spirit is love, joy, peace, longsuffering, gentleness, goodness, faith, meekness, temperance: against such there is no law. Galatians 5:22

And grieve not the holy Spirit of God, whereby ye are sealed unto the day of redemption. Ephesians 4:30

And take the helmet of salvation, and the sword of the Spirit, which is the word of God: Ephesians 6:17

All scripture is given by inspiration of God, and is profitable for doctrine, for reproof, for correction, for instruction in righteousness: 2 Timothy 3:16

But ye have an unction from the Holy One, and ye know all things. 1 John 2:20

But the anointing which ye have received of him abideth in you, and ye need not that any man teach you: but as the same anointing teacheth you of all things, and is truth, and is no lie, and even as it hath taught you, ye shall abide in him. 1 John 2:27

Hereby know ye the Spirit of God: Every spirit that confesseth that Jesus Christ is come in the flesh is of God:
And every spirit that confesseth not that Jesus Christ is come in the flesh is not of God: and this is that spirit of antichrist, whereof ye have heard that it should come; and even now already is it in the world. 1 John 4:2,3

HOMOSEXUALITY

And the rib, which the Lord God had taken from man, made he a woman, and brought her unto the man. Genesis 2:22

Therefore shall a man leave his father and his mother, and shall cleave unto his wife: and they shall be one flesh. Genesis 2:24

Thou shalt not lie with mankind, as with womankind: it is an abomination. Leviticus 18:22

For this cause God gave them up unto vile affections: for even their women did change the natural use into that which is against nature:
And likewise also the men, leaving the natural use of the woman, burned in their lust one toward another; men with men working that which is unseemly, and receiving themselves that recompense of their error which was meet. Romans 1:26,27
Who knowing the judgment of God, that they which commit such things are worthy of death, not only do the same, but have pleasure in them that do them. Romans 1:32

HOROSCOPES

Ye shall not eat anything with the blood: neither shall ye use enchantment, nor observe times. Leviticus 19:26

Regard not them that have familiar spirits, neither seek after wizards, to be defiled by them: I am the Lord your God. Leviticus 19:31

HUMILITY

If my people, which are called by my name, shall humble themselves, and pray, and seek my face, and turn from their wicked ways; then will

I hear from heaven, and will forgive their sin, and will heal their land. 2 Chronicles 7:14

Surely he scorneth the scorners: but he giveth grace unto the lowly. Proverbs 3:34

By humility and the fear of the Lord are riches, and honour, and life. Proverbs 22:4

For thus saith the high and lofty One that inhabiteth eternity, whose name is Holy; I dwell in the high and holy place, with him also that is of a contrite and humble spirit, to revive the spirit of the humble, and to revive the heart of the contrite ones. Isaiah 57:15

Whosoever therefore shall humble himself as this little child, the same is greatest in the kingdom of heaven. Matthew 18:4

I therefore, the prisoner of the Lord, beseech you that ye walk worthy of the vocation wherewith ye are called,
With all lowliness and meekness, with longsuffering, forbearing one another in love; Ephesians 4:1,2

Put on therefore, as the elect of God, holy and beloved, bowels of mercies, kindness, humbleness of mind, meekness, longsuffering; Colossians 3:12

But he giveth more grace. Wherefore he saith, God resisteth the proud, but giveth grace unto the humble. James 4:6

Humble yourselves in the sight of the Lord, and he shall lift you up. James 4:10

Likewise, ye younger, submit yourselves unto the elder. Yea, all of you be subject one to another, and be clothed with humility: for God resisteth the proud, and giveth grace unto the humble.

Humble yourselves therefore under the mighty hand of God, that he may exalt you in due time: 1 Peter 5:5,6

JUDGMENT

Not every one that saith unto me Lord, Lord, shall enter into the kingdom of heaven; but he that doeth the will of my Father which is in heaven. Matthew 7:21

As therefore the tares are gathered and burned in the fire; so shall it be in the end of this world.
The Son of man shall send forth his angels, and they shall gather out of his kingdom all things that offend, and them which do iniquity;
And shall cast them into a furnace of fire: there shall be wailing and gnashing of teeth.
Then shall the righteous shine forth as the sun in the kingdom of their Father. Who hath ears to hear, let him hear. Matthew 13:40-43

He that rejecteth me, and receiveth not my words, hath one that judgeth him: the word that I have spoken, the same shall judge him in the last day. John 12:48

When the Son of man shall come in his glory, and all the holy angels with him, then shall he sit upon the throne of his glory:
And before him shall be gathered all nations: and he shall separate them one from another, as a shepherd divideth his sheep from the goats:
And he shall set the sheep on his right hand, but the goats on the left.
Then shall the King say unto them on his right hand, Come, ye blessed of my Father, inherit the kingdom prepared for you from the foundation of the world: Matthew 25:31-34
Then shall he say unto them on the left hand, Depart from me, ye cursed, into everlasting fire, prepared for the devil and his angels: Matthew 25:41

And these shall go away into everlasting punishment: but the righteous into life eternal. Matthew 25:46

Because he hath appointed a day, in the which he will judge the world in righteousness by that man whom he hath ordained; whereof he hath given assurance unto all men, in that he hath raised him from the dead. Acts 17:31

But after thy hardness and impenitent heart treasurest up unto thyself wrath against the day of wrath and revelation of the righteous judgment of God;
WHO WILL RENDER TO EVERY MAN ACCORDING TO HIS DEEDS. Romans 2:5,6

For as many as have sinned without law shall also perish without law: and as many as have sinned in the law shall be judged by the law; Romans 2:12

In the day when God shall judge the secrets of men by Jesus Christ according to my gospel. Romans 2:16

For we must all appear before the judgment seat of Christ; that every one may receive the things done in his body, according to that he hath done, whether it be good or bad. 2 Corinthians 5:10

And to you who are troubled rest with us, when the Lord Jesus shall be revealed from heaven with his mighty angels,
In flaming fire taking vengeance on them that know not God, and that obey not the gospel of our Lord Jesus Christ:
Who shall be punished with everlasting destruction from the presence of the Lord, and from the glory of his power; 2 Thessalonians 1:7-9

For when they shall say, Peace and safety; then sudden destruction cometh upon them, as travail upon a woman with child; and they shall not escape. 1 Thessalonians 5:3

Henceforth there is laid up for me a crown of righteousness, which the Lord, the righteous judge, shall give me at that day: and not to me only, but unto all them also that love his appearing. 2 Timothy 4:8

And as it is appointed unto men once to die, but after this the judgment: Hebrews 9:27

But the heavens and the earth, which are now, by the same word are kept in store, reserved unto fire against the day of judgment and perdition of ungodly men. 2 Peter 3:7

And I saw the dead, small and great, stand before God; and the books were opened: and another book was opened, which is the book of life: and the dead were judged out of those things which were written in the books, according to their works.
And the sea gave up the dead which were in it; and death and hell delivered up the dead which were in them: and they were judged every man according to their works.
And death and hell were cast into the lake of fire. This is the second death.
And whosoever was not found written in the book of life was cast into the lake of fire. Revelation 20:12-15

How shall we escape, if we neglect so great salvation: which at the first began to be spoken by the Lord, and was confirmed unto us by them that heard him; Hebrews 2:3

But why dost thou judge thy brother? Or why dost thou set at nought thy brother? For we shall all stand before the judgment seat of Christ. Romans 14:10

So then every one of us shall account of himself to God. Romans 14:12

For if after they have escaped the pollutions of the world through the knowledge of the Lord and Saviour Jesus Christ, they are again entangled therein, and overcome, the latter end is worse with them than the beginning.

For it had been better for them not to have known the way of righteousness, than, after they have known it, to turn from the holy commandment delivered unto them. 2 Peter 2:20,21

LAZINESS

And I sent messengers unto them, saying, I am doing a great work, so that I cannot come down: why should the work cease, whilst I leave it, and come down to you? Nehemiah 6:3

By much slothfulness the building decayeth; and through idleness of the hands the house droppeth through. Ecclesiastes 10:18

And they said, Arise, that we may go up against them: for we have seen the land, and, behold, it is very good: and are ye still? Be not slothful to go, and to enter to possess the land. Judges 18:9

Give not sleep to thine eyes, nor slumber to thine eyelids. Proverbs 6:4

Go to the ant, thou sluggard; consider her ways, and be wise: Proverbs 6:6

How long wilt thou sleep, O sluggard? When wilt thou arise out of thy sleep?
Yet a little sleep, a little slumber, a little folding of the hands to sleep:
So shall thy poverty come as one that travelleth, and thy want as an armed man. Proverbs 6:9-11

The hand of the diligent shall bear rule: but the slothful shall be under tribute. Proverbs 12:24

The slothful man roasteth not that which he took in hunting: but the substance of a diligent man is precious. Proverbs 12:27

He also that is slothful in his work is brother to him that is a great waster. Proverbs 18:9

Slothfulness casteth into a deep sleep; and an idle soul shall suffer hunger. Proverbs 19:15

A slothful man hideth his hand in his bosom, and will not so much as bring it to his mouth again. Proverbs 19:24

The sluggard will not plough by reason of the cold; therefore shall he beg in harvest, and have nothing. Proverbs 20:4

The desire of the slothful killeth him; for his hands refuse to labour. Proverbs 21:25

The slothful man saith, There is a lion without, I shall be slain in the streets. Proverbs 22:13

For unto everyone that hath shall be given, and he shall have abundance: but from him that hath not shall be taken away even that which he hath. Matthew 25:29

Not slothful in business; fervent in spirit; serving the Lord; Romans 12:11

For even when we were with you, this we commanded you, that if any would not work, neither should he eat. 2 Thessalonians 3:10

That ye be not slothful, but followers of them who through faith and patience inherit the promises. Hebrews 6:12

LOVE

Jesus said unto him, Thou shalt love the Lord thy God with all thy heart, and with all thy soul, and with all thy mind.
This is the first and greatest commandment.

And the second is like unto it, Thou shalt love thy neighbor as thyself. Matthew 22:37-39

A new commandment I give unto you, That ye love one another; as I have loved you, that ye also love one another.
By this shall all men know that ye are my disciples, if ye have love one to another. John 13:34,35

If ye love me, keep my commandments. John 14:15

Greater love hath no man than this, that a man lay down his life for his friends. John 15:13

He that hath my commandments, and keepeth them, he it is that loveth me: and he that loveth me shall be loved of my Father, and I will love him, and will manifest myself to him. John 14:21

As the Father hath loved me, so have I loved you: continue ye in my love. John 15:9

And hope maketh not ashamed; because the love of God is shed abroad in our hearts by the Holy Ghost which is given unto us. Romans 5:5

But God commendeth his love toward us, in that, while we were yet sinners, Christ died for us. Romans 5:8

And we know that all things work together for good to them that love God, to them who are called according to his purpose. Romans 8:28

Who shall separate us from the love of Christ? shall tribulation, or distress, or persecution, or famine, or nakedness, or peril, or sword? Romans 8:35

Nay, in all things we are more than conquerors through him that loved us.
For I am persuaded, that neither death, nor life, nor angels, nor principalities, nor powers, nor things present, nor things to come,

Nor height, nor depth, nor any other creature, shall be able to separate us from the love of God, which is in Christ Jesus our Lord. Romans 8:37-39

I am crucified with Christ: nevertheless I live; yet not I, but Christ liveth in me: and the life which I now live in the flesh I live by the faith of the Son of God, who loved me, and gave himself for me. Galatians 2:20

Let love be without dissimulation, Abhor that which is evil; cleave to that which is good. Romans 12:9

And now abideth faith, hope, charity, these three; but the greatest of these is charity. 1 Corinthians 13:13

Though I speak with the tongues of men and of angels, and have not charity, I am become as sounding brass, or a tinkling cymbol.
And though I have the gift of prophecy, and understand all mysteries, and all knowledge; and though I have all faith, so that I could remove mountains, and have not charity, I am nothing.
And though I bestow all my goods to feed the poor, and though I give my body to be burned, and have not charity, it profiteth me nothing.
Charity suffereth long, and is kind; charity envieth not; charity vaunteth not itself, is not puffed up, 1 Corinthians 13:1-4

But God, who is rich in mercy, for his great love wherewith he loved us,
Even when we were dead in sins, hath quickened us together with Christ, (by grace ye are saved;) Ephesians 2:4,5

And to know the love of Christ, which passeth knowledge, that ye might be filled with the fulness of God. Ephesians 3:19

That Christ may dwell in your hearts by faith; that ye, being rooted and grounded in love, Ephesians 3:17

And walk in love, as Christ also hath loved us, and hath given himself for us an offering and a sacrifice to God for a sweetsmelling savour. Ephesians 5:2

Husbands, love your wives, even as Christ also loved the church, and gave himself for it; Ephesians 5:25

So ought men to love their wives as their own bodies. He that loveth his wife loveth himself. Ephesians 5:28

Nevertheless let every one of you in particular so love his wife even as himself; and the wife see that she reverence her husband. Ephesians 5:33

But whoso keepeth his word, in him verily is the love of God perfected: hereby know we that we are in him. 1 John 2:5

Love not the world, neither the things that are in the world. If any man love the world, the love of the Father is not in him. 1 John 2:15

My little children, let us not love in word, neither in tongue; but in deed and in truth. 1 John 3:18

Let all your things be done with charity. 1 Corinthians 16:14

Keep yourselves in the love of God, looking for the mercy of our Lord Jesus Christ unto eternal life. Jude 21

LUST

But I say unto you, That whosoever looketh on a woman to lust after her hath committed adultery with her already in his heart. Matthew 5:28

But those things which proceed out of the mouth come forth from the heart; and they defile the man. Matthew 15:18

This I say then, Walk in the Spirit, and ye shall not fulfill the lust of the flesh.
For the flesh lusteth against the Spirit, and the Spirit against the flesh: and these are contrary the one to the other: so that ye cannot do the things that ye would. Galatians 5:16-17

That ye put off concerning the former conversation the old man, which is corrupt according to the deceitful lusts; Ephesians 4:22

But they that will be rich fall into temptation and a snare, and into many foolish hurtful lusts, which drown men in destruction and perdition. 1 Timothy 6:9

Flee also youthful lusts: but follow righteousness, faith, charity, peace, with them that call on the Lord out of a pure heart. 2 Timothy 2:22

Having a form of godliness, but denying the power thereof: from such turn away.
For of this sort are they which creep into houses, and lead captive silly women laden with sins, led away with divers lusts, 2 Timothy 3:5,6

For the time will come when they will not endure sound doctrine; but after their own lusts shall they heap to themselves teachers, having itching ears;
And they shall turn away their ears from the truth, and shall be turned unto fables. 2 Timothy 4:3,4

But every man is tempted, when he is drawn away of his own lust, and enticed.
Then when lust hath conceived, it bringeth forth sin: and sin, when it is finished, bringeth forth death. James 1:14,15

Teaching us that, denying ungodliness and worldly lusts, we should live soberly, righteously, and godly in this present world; Titus 2:12

Whereby are given unto us exceeding great and precious promises: that by these ye might be partakers of the divine nature, having escaped the corruption that is in the world through lust. 2 Peter 1:4

Knowing this first, that there shall come in the last days scoffers, walking after their own lusts, 2 Peter 3:3

MARRIAGE

And the Lord God said, It is not good that the man should be alone; I will make him an help meet for him. Genesis 2:18

And the rib, which the Lord God had taken from man, made he a woman, and brought her unto the man. Genesis 2:22

Therefore shall a man leave his father and his mother, and shall cleave unto his wife: and they shall be one flesh. Genesis 2:24

And all thy children shall be taught of the Lord; and great shall be the peace of thy children. Isaiah 54:13

And these words, which I command thee this day, shall be in thine heart:
And thou shalt teach them diligently unto thy children, and shalt talk of them when thou sittest in thine house, and when thou walkest by the way, and when thou liest down, and when thou risest up. Deuteronomy 6:6,7

And thou shalt bind them for a sign upon thine hand, and they shall be as fauntlets between thine eyes. Deuteronomy 6:8

And thou shalt write them upon the posts of thy house, and on thy gates. Deuteronomy 6:9

What ye know, the same do I know also; I am not inferior unto you. Job 13:2

O that ye would altogether hold your peace! And it should be your wisdom.
Hear now my reasoning, and hearken to the pleadings of my lips. Job 13:5,6

Hearken, O daughter, and consider, and incline thine ear; forget also thine own people, and thy father's house; Psalm 45:10

Except the Lord build the house, they labour in vain that build it: except the Lord keep the city, the watchman waketh but in vain. Psalm 127:1

Lo, children are an heritage of the Lord: and the fruit of the womb is his reward. Psalm 127:3

Thy wife shall be as a fruitful vine by the sides of thine house: thy children like olive plants round about thy table. Psalm 128:3

Drink waters out of thine own cistern, and running waters out of thine own well.
Let thy fountains be dispersed abroad, and rivers of waters in the streets.
Let them be only thine own, and not strangers' with thee.
Let thou fountain be blessed: and rejoice with the wife of thy youth.
Let her be as the loving hind and pleasant roe; let her breast satisfy thee at all times; and be thou ravished always with her love.
And why wilt thou, my son, be ravished with a strange woman, and embrace the bosom of a stranger? Proverbs 5:15-20

A good man leaveth an inheritance to his children's children: and the wealth of the sinner is laid up for the just. Proverbs 13:22

A good man obtaineth favour of the Lord: but a man of wicked devices will he condemn. Proverbs 12:2

A virtuous woman is a crown to her husband: but she that maketh ashamed is as rottenness in his bones. Proverbs 12:4

Better is a dinner of herbs where love is, than a stalled ox and hatred therewith. Proverbs 15:17

A violent man inticeth his neighbor, and leadeth him into the way that is not good. Proverbs 16:29

Better is a dry morsal, and quietness therewith, than a house full of sacrifices with strife. Proverbs 17:1

A brother offended is harder to be won than a strong city: and their contentions are like the bars of a castle. Proverbs 18:19

Whoso findeth a wife findeth a good thing, and obtaineth favor of the Lord. Proverbs 18:22

A foolish son is the calamity of his father: and the contentions of a wife are a continual dropping. Proverbs 19:13

House and riches are the inheritance of fathers: and a prudent wife is from the Lord. Proverbs 19:14

A soft answer turneth away wrath: but grievous words stir up anger. Proverbs 15:1

It is better to dwell in a corner of the housetop, than with a brawling woman in a wide house. Proverbs 21:9

It is better to dwell in the wilderness, than with a contentious and an angry woman. Proverbs 21:19

Train up a child in the way he should go: and when he is old, he will not depart from it. Proverbs 22:6

Make no friendship with an angry man; and with a furious man thou shalt not go;
Lest thou learn his ways, and get a snare to thy soul. Proverbs 22:24,25

A fool uttereth all his mind: but a wise man keepeth it in till afterwards. Proverbs 29:11

Who can find a virtuous woman? For her price is far above rubies.
The heart of her husband doth safely trust in her, so that he shall have no need of spoil.
She will do him good and not evil all the days of her life. Proverbs 31:10-12

Her children arise up, and call her blessed; her husband also, and he praiseth her. Proverbs 31:28

Favour is deceitful, and beauty is vain: but a woman that feareth the Lord, she shall be praised. Proverbs 31:30

Take us the foxes, the little foxes, that spoil the vines: for our vines have tender grapes. Songs of Solomon 2:15

Can two walk together, except they be agreed? Amos 3:3

Yet ye say, Wherefore? Because the Lord hath been witness between thee and the wife of thy youth, against whom thou hast dealt treacherously: yet is she thy companion, and the wife of thy covenant.
And did not he make one? Yet he had the residue of the spirit. And wherefore one? That he might seek a godly seed. Therefore take heed to your spirit, and let known deal treacherously against the wife of his youth. Malachi 2:14,15

Again I say unto you, That if two of you shall agree on earth as touching any thing that they shall ask, it shall be done for them of my Father which is in heaven. Matthew 18:19

Wherefore they are no more twain, but one flesh. What therefore God hath joined together, let no man put asunder. Matthew 19.6

And if a house be divided against itself, that house cannot stand. Mark 3:25

Be ye angry, and sin not: let not the sun go down upon your wrath: Neither give place to the devil. Ephesians 4:26,27

For the woman which hath an husband is bound by the law to her husband so long as he liveth; but if the husband be dead, she is loosed from the law of her husband. Romans 7:2

Be kindly affectioned one to another with brotherly love; in honour preferring one another. Romans 12:10

Now concerning the things whereof ye wrote unto me: It is good for a man not to touch a woman.
Nevertheless, to avoid fornication, let every man have his own wife, and let every woman have her own husband.
Let the husband render unto the wife due benevolence: and likewise also the wife unto the husband.
The wife hath not power of her own body, but the husband: and likewise also the husband hath not power of his own body, but the wife.
Defraud ye not one the other, except it be with consent for a time, that ye may give yourselves to fasting and prayer; and come together again, that Satan tempt you not for your incontinency. 1 Corinthians 7:1-5

Be ye not unequally yoked together with unbelievers: for what fellowship hath righteousness with unrighteousness? And what communion hath light with darkness? 2 Corinthians 6:14

Let no corrupt communication proceed out of your mouth, but that which is good to the use of edifying, that it may minister grace unto the hearers. Ephesians 4:29

And be ye kind one to another, tenderhearted, forgiving one another, even as God for Christ's sake hath forgiven you. Ephesians 4:32

Submitting yourselves one to another in the fear of God. Ephesians 5:21

Husbands, love your wives, even as Christ also loved the church, and gave himself for it. Ephesians 5:25

Wives, submit yourselves unto your own husbands, as unto the Lord. For the husband is the head of the wife, even as Christ is the head of the church: and he is the saviour of the body.
Therefore as the church is subject unto Christ, so let the wives be to their own husbands in every thing. Ephesians 5:22-24

Nevertheless let every one of you in particular so love his wife even as himself; and the wife see that she reverence her husband. Ephesians 5:33

And, ye fathers, provoke not your children to wrath: but bring them up in the nurture and admonition of the Lord. Ephesians 6:4

Wives, submit yourselves unto your own husbands, as it is fit in the Lord. Colossians 3:18

Husbands, love your wives, and be not bitter against them. Colossians 3:19

Fathers, provoke not your children to anger, lest they be discouraged. Colossians 3:21

But if any provide not for his own, and specially for those of his own house, he hath denied the faith, and is worse than an infidel. 1 Timothy 5:8

That they may teach the young women to be sober, to love their husbands, to love their children,

To be discreet, chaste, keepers at home, good, obedient to their own husbands, that the word of God be not blasphemed.
Young men likewise exhort to be sober minded. Titus 2:4-6

Marriage is honourable in all, and the bed undefiled: but whoremongers and adulterers God will judge. Hebrews 13:4

Likewise, ye wives, be in subjection to your own husbands; that, if any obey not the word, they also may without the word be won by the conversation of the wives. 1 Peter 3:1

For after this manner in the old time the holy women also, who trusted in God, adorned themselves, being in subjection unto their own husbands: 1 Peter 3:5

Likewise, ye husbands, dwell with them according to knowledge, giving honour unto the wife, as unto the weaker vessel, and as being heirs together of the grace of life; that your prayers be not hindered. 1 Peter 3:7

PASTORS

And he said unto him, Behold now, there is in this city a man of God, and he is an honorable man; all that he saith cometh surely to pass: now let us go thither; peradventure he can shew us our way that we should go.
Then said Saul to his servant, But, behold, if we go, what shall we bring the man? For the bread is spent in our vessels, and there is not a present to bring the man of God: what have we?
And the servant answered Saul again, and said, Behold, I have here at hand the fourth part of a shekel of silver: that will I give to the man of God, to tell us our way. 1 Samuel 9:6-8

…Believe in the Lord your God, so shall ye be established; believe his prophets, so shall ye prosper. 2 Chronicles 20:20

And I will give you pastors according to mine heart, which shall feed you with knowledge and understanding. Jeremiah 3:15

Woe be unto the pastors that destroy and scatter the sheep of my pasture! Saith the Lord. Jeremiah 23:1

He that receiveth a prophet in the name of a prophet shall receive a prophet's reward; and he that receiveth a righteous man in the name of a righteous man shall receive a righteous man's reward. Matthew 10:41

For the priest's lips should keep knowledge, and they should seek the law at his mouth: for he is the messenger of the Lord of hosts. Malachi 2:7

Carry neither purse, nor scrip, nor shoes: and salute no man by the way. Luke 10:4

And in the same house remain, eating and drinking such things as they give: for the labourer is worthy of his hire. Go not from that house. Luke 10:7

How then shall they call on him in whom they have not believed? And how shall they believe in him of whom they have not heard? And how shall they hear without a preacher.
And how shall they preach, except they be sent? As it is written, How beautiful are the feet of them that preach the gospel of peace, and bring glad tidings of good things! Romans 10:14,15

Let him who is taught the word share in all good things with him who teaches. Galatians 6:6 NKJV

Who ever goes to war at his own expense? Who plants a vineyard and does not eat of its fruit? Or who tends a flock and does not drink of the milk of the flock? 1 Corinthians 9:7 NKJV

If we have sown unto you spiritual things, is it a great thing if we shall reap your carnal things? 1 Corinthians 9:11

Do ye not know that they which minister about holy things live of the things of the temple? And they which wait at the altar are partakers with the altar? 1 Corinthians 9:13

Even so hath the Lord ordained that they which preach the gospel should live of the gospel. 1 Corinthians 9:14

Not because I desire a gift: but I desire fruit that may abound to your account. Philippians 4:17

Let the elders that rule well be counted worthy of double honour, especially they who labor in the word and doctrine.
For the scripture saith, Thou shalt not muzzle the ox that treadeth out the corn. And, the labourer is worthy of his reward. 1 Timothy 5:17,18

And the first of all the firstfruits of all things, and every oblation of all, of every sort of your oblations, shall be the priest's: ye shall also give unto the priest the first of your dough, that he may cause the blessing to rest in thine house. Ezekiel 44:30

Saying, touch not mine anointed, and do my prophets no harm. Psalm 105:15

And he gave some, apostles; and some, prophets; and some, evangelists; and some, pastors and teachers;
For the perfecting of the saints, for the work of the ministry, for the edifying of the body of Christ: Ephesians 4:11,12

And without all contradiction the less is blessed of the better. Hebrew 7:7

PATIENCE

And not only so, but we glory in tribulations also, knowing that tribulation worketh patience; Romans 5:3

But if we hope for that we see not, then do we with patience wait for it. Romans 8:25

For whatsoever things were written aforetime were written for our learning, that we through patience and comfort of the scriptures might have hope.
Now the God of patience and consolation grant you to be likeminded one toward another according to Christ Jesus: Romans 15:4,5

Knowing this, that the trying of your faith worketh patience.
But let patience have her perfect work, that ye may be perfect and entire, wanting nothing. James 1:3,4

Be patience therefore, brethren, unto the coming of the Lord. Behold, the husbandman waiteth for the precious fruit of the earth, and hath long patience for it, until he receive the early and latter rain.
Be ye also patient; stablish your hearts: for the coming of the Lord draweth nigh. James 5:7,8

Do all things without murmurings and disputings: Philippians 2:14

As so, after he had patiently endured, he obtained the promise. Hebrews 6:15

PEACE

I will both lay me down in peace, and sleep: for thou, Lord, only makest me dwell in safety. Psalm 4:8

The Lord will give strength unto his people; the Lord will bless his people with peace. Psalm 29:11

But the meek shall inherit the earth; and shall delight themselves in the abundance of peace. Psalm 37:11

Mark the perfect man, and behold the upright: for the end of that man is peace. Psalm 37:37

He maketh peace in thy borders, and filleth thee with the finest of the wheat. Psalm 147:14

When a man's ways please the Lord, he maketh even his enemies to be at peace with him. Proverbs 16:7

For unto us a child is born, unto us a son is given: and the government shall be upon his shoulder: and his name shall be Wonderful, Counsellor, The mighty God, The everlasting Father, The Prince of Peace. Isaiah 9:6

Thou wilt keep him in perfect peace, whose mind is stayed on thee: because he trusteth in thee. Isaiah 26:3

Lord, thou wilt ordain peace for us: for thou also hast wrought all our works in us. Isaiah 26:12

Come unto me, all ye that labour and are heavy laden, and I will give you rest. Matthew 11:28

And he said unto her, Daughter, be of good comfort: thy faith hath made thee whole; go in peace. Luke 8:48

Peace I leave with you, my peace I give unto you: not as the world giveth, give I unto you. Let not your heart be troubled, neither let it be afraid. John 14:27

These things I have spoken unto you, that in me ye might have peace. In the world ye shall have tribulation: but be of good cheer; I have overcome the world. John 16:33

Therefore being justified by faith, we have peace with God through our Lord Jesus Christ: Romans 5:1

For to be carnally minded is death; but to be spiritually minded is life and peace. Romans 8:6

Let us therefore follow after the things which make for peace, and things wherewith one may edify another. Romans 14:19

Now the God of hope fill you with all joy and peace in believing, that ye may abound in hope, through the power of the Holy Ghost. Romans 15:13

But if the unbelieving depart, let him depart. A brother or a sister is not under bondage in such cases: But God hath called us to peace. 1 Corinthians 7:15

Finally, brethren, farewell. Be perfect, be of good comfort, be of one mind, live in peace; and the God of love and peace shall be with you. 2 Corinthians 13:11

And the peace of God, which passeth all understanding, shall keep your hearts and minds through Christ Jesus. Philippians 4:7

Those things, which ye have both learned, and received, and heard, and seen in me, do: and the God of peace shall be with you. Philippians 4:9

And, having made peace through the blood of his cross, by him to reconcile all things unto himself; by him, I say, whether they be things in the earth, or things in heaven. Colossians 1:20

And let the peace of God rule in your hearts, to the which also ye are called in one body; and be ye thankful. Colossians 3:15

Flee also youthful lust: but follow righteousness, faith, charity, peace with them that call on the Lord out of a pure heart. 2 Timothy 2:22

Follow peace with all men, and holiness, without which no man shall see the Lord: Hebrews 12:14

There remaineth therefore a rest to the people of God.
For he that is entered into his rest, he also hath ceased from his own works, as God did from his.
Let us labour therefore to enter into that rest, lest any man fall after the same example of unbelief. Hebrews 4:9-11

PRAYER

For this shall every one that is godly pray unto thee in a time when thou mayest be found: surely in the floods of great waters they shall not come nigh unto him. Psalm 32:6

If I regard iniquity in my heart, the Lord will not hear me:
But verily God hath heard me; he hath attended to the voice of my prayer.
Blessed be God, which hath not turned away my prayer, nor his mercy from me. Psalm 66:18-20

And when thou prayest, thou shalt not be as the hypocrites are: for they love to pray standing in the synagogues and in the corners of the streets, that they may be seen of men. Verily I say unto you, They have their reward. Matthew 6:5

But thou, when thou prayest, enter into thy closet, and when thou hast shut the door, pray to thy Father which is in secret; and thy Father which seeth in secret shall reward thee openly. Matthew 6:6

But when ye pray, use not vain repetitions, as the heathen do: for they think that they shall be heard for their much speaking. Matthew 6:7

And when he had sent the multitudes away, he went up into a mountain apart to pray: and when the evening was come, he was there alone. Matthew 14:23

Again I say unto you, That if two of you shall agree on earth as touching anything that they shall ask, it shall be done for them of my Father which is in heaven.
For where two or three are gathered together in my name, there am I in the midst of them. Matthew 18:19,20

And all things, whatsoever ye shall ask in prayer, believing, ye shall receive. Matthew 21:22

And in the morning, rising up a great while before day, he went out, and departed into a solitary place, and there prayed. Mark 1:35

Therefore I say unto you, What things soever ye desire, when ye pray, believe that ye receive them, and ye shall have them. Mark 11:24

And when ye stand praying, forgive; if ye have ought against any: that your Father also which is in heaven may forgive you your trespasses. Mark 11:25

Watch ye and pray, lest ye enter into temptation. The spirit truly is ready, but the flesh is weak. Mark 14:38

And he spake a parable unto them to this end, that men ought to always to pray, and not to faint; Luke 18:1

If ye shall ask anything in my name, I will do it. John 14:14

What is it then? I will pray with the spirit, and I will pray with the understanding also: I will sing with the spirit, and I will sing with the understanding also. 1 Corinthians 14:15

Pray without ceasing. 1 Thessalonians 5:17

Be careful for nothing; but in everything by prayer and supplication with thanksgiving let your request be made known unto God. Philippians 4:6

Likewise the Spirit also helpeth our infirmities: for we know not what we should pray for as we ought: but the Spirit itself maketh intercession for us with groanings which cannot be uttered. Romans 8:26

Continue in prayer, and watch in the same with thanksgiving; Colossians 4:2

Praying always with all prayer and supplication in the Spirit, and watching thereunto with all perseverance and supplication for all saints; Ephesians 6:18

And he withdrew himself into the wilderness, and prayed. Luke 5:16

I exhort therefore, that, first of all, supplications, prayers, intercessions, and giving of thanks, be made for all men;
For kings, and for all that are in authority; that we may lead a quiet and peaceable life in all godliness and honesty. 1 Timothy 2:1,2

I will therefore that men pray every where, lifting up holy hands, without wrath and doubting. 1 Timothy 2:8

But ye, beloved, building up yourselves on your most holy faith, praying in the Holy Ghost, Jude 20

And this is the confidence that we have in him, that, if we ask anything according to his will, he heareth us:
And if we know that he hear us, whatsoever we ask, we know that we have the petitions that we desired of him. 1 John 5:14,15

Is any among you afflicted? Let him pray. Is any merry? Let him sing psalms.

Is any sick among you? Let him call for the elders of the church; and let them pray over him, anointing him with oil in the name of the Lord: And the prayer of faith shall save the sick, and the Lord shall raise him up; and if he have committed sins, they shall be forgiven him.
Confess your faults one to another, and pray one for another, that ye may be healed. The effectual fervent prayer of a righteous man availeth much. James 5:13-16

THE PRESENCE OF GOD

Know therefore this day, and consider it in thine heart, that the Lord he is God in heaven above and upon the earth beneath: there is none else. Deuteronomy 4:39

Be strong and of good courage, fear not, nor be afraid of them: for the Lord thy God, he it is that doth go with thee; he will not fail thee, nor forsake thee. Deuteronomy 31:6

Shall not God search this out? For he knoweth the secrets of the heart. Psalm 44:21

O Lord, thou hast searched me, and known me.
Thou knowest my downsitting and mine uprising, thou understandest my thought afar off. Psalm 139:1,2

Thou compassest my path and my lying down, and art acquainted with all my ways. Psalm 139:3

For there is not a word in my tongue, but, lo, O Lord, thou knowest it all together. Psalm 139:4

Whither shall I go from thy spirit? Or whither shall I flee from thy presence? Psalm 139:7

If I ascend up into heaven, thou art there: if I make my bed in hell, behold thou art there. Psalm 139:8

If I take the wings of the morning, and dwell in the uttermost parts of the sea;
Even there shall thy hand lead me, and thy right hand shall hold me. Psalm 139:9,10

If I say, Surely the darkness shall cover me; even the night shall be light about me. Psalm 139:11

Yea, the darkness hideth not from thee; but the night shineth as the day: the darkness and the light are both alike to thee. Psalm 139:12

For thou hast possessed my reins: thou hast covered me in my mother's womb. Psalm 139:13

The eyes of the Lord are in every place, beholding the evil and the good. Proverbs 15:3

Am I a God at hand, saith the Lord, and not a God afar off?
Can any hide himself in secret places that I shall not see him? Saith the Lord. Do not I fill heaven and earth? Saith the Lord. Jeremiah 23:23,24

Teaching them to observe all things whatsoever I have commanded you: and; lo, I am with you alway, even unto the end of the world. Matthew 28:20

For the word of God is quick, and powerful, and sharper than any twoedged sword, piercing even to the dividing of asunder of soul and spirit, and of the joints and marrow, and is a discerner of the thoughts and intents of the heart. Hebrews 4:12

Neither is there any creature that is not manifest in his sight: but all things are naked and opened unto the eyes of him with whom we have to do. Hebrews 4:13

For the ways of man are before the eyes of the Lord, and he pondereth all his goings. Proverbs 5:21

PROMISED BLESSINGS OF OBEDIENCE

And it shall come to pass, if thou shalt hearken diligently unto the voice of the Lord thy God, to observe and to do all his commandments which I command thee this day, that the Lord thy God will set thee on high above all nations of the earth: Deuteronomy 28:1

And all these blessings shall come on thee, and overtake thee if thou wilt hearken unto the voice of the Lord thy God. Deuteronomy 28:2

Blessed shalt thou be in the city, and blessed shalt thou be in the field. Deuteronomy 28:3

Blessed shall be the fruit of thy body, and the fruit of thy ground, and the fruit of thy cattle, the increase of thy kine, and the flocks of thy sheep. Deuteronomy 28:4

Blessed shall be thy basket and thy store. Deuteronomy 28:5

Blessed shalt thou be when thou comest in, and blessed shalt thou be when thou goest out. Deuteronomy 28:6

The Lord shall cause thine enemies that rise up against thee to be smitten before thy face: they shall come out against thee one way, and flee before thee seven ways. Deuteronomy 28:7

The Lord shall command the blessing upon thee in thy storehouses, and in all that thou settest thine hand unto; and he shall bless thee in the land which the Lord thy God giveth thee. Deuteronomy 28:8

The Lord shall establish thee an holy people unto himself, as he hath sworn unto thee, if thou shalt keep the commandments of the Lord thy God, and walk in his ways. Deuteronomy 28:9

And all people of the earth shall see that thou art called by the name of the Lord; and they shall be afraid of thee. Deuteronomy 28:10

And the Lord shall make thee plenteous in goods, in the fruit of thy body, and in the fruit of thy cattle, and in the fruit of thy ground, in the land which the Lord sware unto thy fathers to give thee. Deuteronomy 28:11

The Lord shall open unto thee his good treasure, the heaven to give the rain unto thy land in his season, and to bless all the work of thine hand: and thou shalt lend to many nations, and thou shalt not borrow. Deuteronomy 28:12

And the Lord shall make thee the head, and not the tail; and thou shalt be above only, and thou shalt not be beneath; if that thou hearken unto the commandments of the Lord thy God, which I command thee this day, to observe and to do them: Deuteronomy 28:13

PROSPERITY

But thou shalt remember the Lord thy God: for it is he that giveth thee power to get wealth, that he may establish his covenant which he sware unto thy fathers, as it is this day. Deuteronomy 8:18

Praise ye the Lord. Blessed is the man that feareth the Lord, that delighteth greatly in his commandments.

His seed shall be mighty upon earth: the generation of the upright shall be blessed.

Wealth and riches shall be in his house: and his righteousness endureth for ever. Psalm 112:1-3

The Lord shall increase you more and more, you and your children. Psalm 115:14

For thou shalt eat the labour of thine hands: happy shalt thou be, and it shall be well with thee. Psalm 128:2

And they rose early in the morning, and went forth into the wilderness of Tekoa: and as they went forth, Jehoshaphat stood and said, Hear me, O Judah, and ye inhabitants of Jerusalem; Believe in the Lord your God, so shall ye be established; believe his prophets, so shall ye prosper. 2 Chronicles 20:20

And in every work that he began in the service of the house of God, and in the law, and in the commandments, to seek his God, he did it with all his heart, and prospered. 2 Chronicles 31:21

Only be thou strong and very courageous, that thou mayest observe to do according to all the law, which Moses my servant commanded thee: turn not from it to the right hand or to the left, that thou mayest prosper whithersoever thou goest. Joshua 1:7

This book of the law shall not depart out of thy mouth; but thou shalt meditate therein day and night, that thou mayest observe to do according to all that is written therein: for then thou shalt make thy way prosperous, and then thou shalt have good success. Joshua 1:8

And he shall be like a tree planted by the rivers of water, that bringeth forth his fruit in his season; his leaf also shall not whither; and whatsoever he doeth shall prosper. Psalm 1:3

Let them shout for joy, and be glad, that favour my righteous cause: yea, let them say continually, Let the Lord be magnified, which hath pleasure in the prosperity of his servant. Psalm 35:27

The blessing of the Lord, it maketh rich, and he addeth no sorrow with it. Proverbs 10:22

A gift is as a precious stone in the eyes of him that hath it: whithersoever it turneth, it prospereth. Proverbs 17:8

Now unto him that is able to do exceeding abundantly above all that we ask or think, according to the power that worketh in us, Ephesians 3:20

Charge them that are rich in this world, that they be not highminded, nor trust in uncertain riches, but in the living God, who giveth us richly all things to enjoy; 1 Timothy 6:17

Beloved, I wish above all things that thou mayest prosper and be in health, even as thy soul prospereth. 3 John 2

Blessed is he that readeth, and they that hear the words of this prophecy, and keep those things which are written therein: for the time is at hand. Revelation 1:3

…Not by might, nor by power, but by my spirit, saith the Lord of hosts. Zechariah 4:6

PROTECTION

There shall not any man be able to stand before thee all the days of thy life: as I was with Moses, so I will be with thee: I will not fail thee, nor forsake thee. Joshua 1:5

Hast not thou made an hedge about him, and about his house, and about all that he hath on every side? Thou hast blessed the work of his hands, and his substance is increased in the land. Job 1:10

I laid me down and slept; I awaked; for the Lord sustained me. Psalm 3:5

I will both lay me down in peace, and sleep: for thou, Lord, only makest me dwell in safety. Psalm 4:8

Ye, though I walk through the valley of the shadow of death, I will fear no evil: for thou art with me: thy rod and thy staff they comfort me. Psalm 23:4

When I cry unto thee, then shall mine enemies turn back; this I know; for God is for me. Psalm 56:9

For thou hast delivered my soul from death: wilt not thou deliver my feet from falling, that I may walk before God in the light of the living. Psalm 56:13

He that dwelleth in the secret place of the most High shall abide under the shadow of the Almighty.
I will say of the Lord, He is my refuge and my fortress: my God; in him will I trust.
Surely he shall deliver me from the snare of the fowler, and from the noisome pestilence.
He shall cover thee with his feathers, and under his wings shalt thou trust: his truth shall be thy shield and buckler.
Thou shalt not be afraid for the terror by night; nor for the arrow that flieth by day;
Nor for the pestilence that walketh in darkness; nor for the destruction that wasteth at noonday.
A thousand shall fall at thy side, and ten thousand at thy right hand; but it shall not come nigh thee.

Only with thine eyes shalt thou behold and see the reward of the wicked.

Because thou hast made the Lord, which is my refuge, even the most High, thy habitation;

There shall no evil befall thee, neither shall any plague come nigh thy dwelling.

For he shall give his angels charge over thee, to keep thee in all thy ways.

They shalt bear thee up in their hands, lest thou dash thy foot against a stone.

Thou shalt tread upon the lion and adder: the young lion and the dragon shalt thou trample under feet.

Because he hath set his love upon me, therefore will I deliver him: I will set him on high, because he hath known my name.

He shall call upon me, and I will answer him: I will be with him in trouble; I will deliver him, and honour him.

With long life will I satisfy him, and shew him my salvation. Psalm 91

Then they cry unto the Lord in their trouble, and he saveth them out of their distresses. Psalm 107:19

I will lift up mine eyes unto the hills, from whence cometh my help.

My help cometh from the Lord, which made heaven and earth.

He will not suffer thy foot to be moved: he that keepeth thee will not slumber.

Behold, he that keepeth Israel shall neither slumber nor sleep.

The Lord is thy keeper: the Lord is thy shade upon thy right hand.

The sun shall not smite thee by day, nor the moon by night.

The Lord shall preserve thee from all evil: he shall preserve thy soul.

The Lord shall preserve thy going out and thy coming in from this time forth, and even for evermore. Psalm 121:1-8

The name of the Lord is a strong tower: the righteous runneth into it, and is safe. Proverbs 18:10

Fear thou not; for I am with thee: be not dismayed; for I am thy God: I will strengthen thee; yea, I will help thee; yea, I will uphold thee with the right hand of my righteousness. Isaiah 41:10

No weapon that is formed against thee shall prosper; and every tongue that shall rise against thee in judgment thou shalt condemn. This is the heritage of the servants of the Lord, and their righteousness is of me, saith the Lord. Isaiah 54:17

What shall we then say to these things? If God be for us, who can be against us. Romans 8:31

My Father, which gave them me, is greater than all; and no man is able to pluck them out of my Father's hand. John 10:29

But the Lord is faithful, who shall stablish you, and keep you from evil. 2 Thessalonians 3:3

Because thou hast kept the word of my patience, I also will keep thee from the hour of temptation, which shall come upon all the world, to try them that dwell upon the earth. Revelation 3:10

THE RAPTURE

For the Son of man shall come in the glory of his Father with his angels; and then he shall reward every man according to his works. Matthew 16:27

And this gospel of the kingdom shall be preached in all the world for a witness unto all nations; and then shall the end come. Matthew 24:14

For as the lightning cometh out of the east, and shineth even unto the west; so shall also the coming of the Son of man be. Matthew 24:27

But of that day and hour knoweth no man, no, not even the angels of heaven, but my Father only. Matthew 24:36

But as the days of Noe were, so shall also the coming of the Son of man be.
For as in the days that were before the flood they were eating and drinking, marrying and giving in marriage, until the day that Noe entered into the ark,
And knew not until the flood came, and took them all away; so shall also the coming of the Son of man be.
Then shall two be in the field; the one shall be taken, and the other left.
Two women shall be grinding at the mill; the one shall be taken, and the other left.
Watch therefore; for ye know not what hour your Lord doth come. Matthew 24:37-42

Therefore be ye also ready: for in such an hour as ye think not the Son of man cometh. Matthew 24:44

Watch therefore, for ye know neither the day nor the hour wherein the Son of man cometh. Matthew 25:13

And if I go and prepare a place for you, I will come again, and receive you unto myself; that where I am, there ye may be also. John 14:3

The last enemy that shall be destroyed is death. 1 Corinthians 15:26

Behold, I shew you a mystery; We shall not all sleep, but we shall all be changed,
In a moment, in the twinkling of an eye, at the last trump: for the trumpet shall sound, and the dead shall be raised incorruptible, and we shall be changed.
For this corruptible must put on incorruption, and this mortal must put on immortality.

So when this corruptible shall have put on incorruption, and this mortal shall have put on immortality, then shall be brought to pass the saying that is written, Death is swallowed up in victory. 1 Corinthians 15:51-54

When Christ, who is our life, shall appear, then shall ye also appear with him in glory. Colossians 3:4

For if we believe that Jesus died and rose again, even so them also which sleep in Jesus will God bring with him.
For this we say unto you by the word of the Lord, that we which are alive and remain unto the coming of the Lord shall not prevent them which are asleep.
For the Lord himself shall descend from heaven with a shout, with the voice of the archangel, and with the trump of God: and the dead in Christ shall rise first:
Then we which are alive and remain shall be caught up together with them in the clouds, to meet the Lord in the air: and so shall we ever be with the Lord.
Wherefore comfort one another with these words. 1 Thessalonians 4: 14-18

For yourselves know perfectly that the day of the Lord so cometh as a thief in the night.
For when they shall say, Peace and safety; then sudden destruction cometh upon them, as travail upon a woman with child; and they shall not escape.
But ye, brethren, are not in darkness, that that day should overtake you as a thief. 1 Thessalonians 5:2-4

Therefore let us not sleep, as do others; but let us watch and be sober. 1 Thessalonians 5:6

Henceforth there is laid up for me a crown of righteousness, which the Lord, the righteous judge, shall give me at that day: and not to me only, but unto all them also that love his appearing. 2 Timothy 4:8

THE RESURRECTION

God is not a man, that he should lie; neither the son of man, that he should repent: hath he said, and shall he not do it? Or hath he spoken, and shall he not make it good? Numbers 23:19

For thou wilt not leave my soul in hell; neither wilt thou suffer thine Holy One to see corruption. Psalm 16:10

Thy dead men shall live, together with my dead body shall they arise. Awake and sing, ye that dwell in dust: for thy dew is as the dew of herbs, and the earth shall cast out the dead. Isaiah 26:19

From that time forth began Jesus to shew unto his disciples, how that he must go unto Jerusalem, and suffer many things of the elders and chief priests and scribes, and be killed, and be raised again the third day. Matthew 16:21

Then saith Jesus unto them, All ye shall be offended because of me this night: for it is written, I will smite the shepherd, and the sheep of the flock shall be scattered abroad.
But after I am risen again, I will go before you into Galilee. Matthew 26:31,32

In the end of the sabbath, as it began to dawn toward the first day of the week, came Mary Magdelene and the other Mary to see the sepulchre. Matthew 28:1
And the angel answered and said unto the women, Fear not ye: for I know that ye seek Jesus, which was crucified.
He is not here: for he is risen, as he said. Come, see the place where the Lord lay. Matthew 28:5,6

Jesus answered and said unto them, Destroy this temple, and in three days I will raise it up. John 2:19
But he spake of the temple of his body.

When therefore he was risen from the dead, his disciples remembered that he had said this unto them; and they believed the scripture, and the word which Jesus had said. John 2:21,22

To whom also he shewed himself alive after his passion by many infallible proofs, being seen of them forty days, and speaking of the things pertaining to the kingdom of God: Acts 1:3

But now is Christ risen from the dead, and become the firstfruits of them that slept.
For since by man came death, by man came also the resurrection of the dead.
For as in Adam all die, even so in Christ shall all be made alive. 1 Corinthians 15:20-22.

RIGHTEOUSNESS

In the way of righteousness is life; and in the pathway thereof there is no death. Proverbs 12:28

In righteousness shalt thou be established: thou shalt be far from oppression; for thou shalt not fear: and from terror; for it shall not come near thee. Isaiah 54:14

But we are all as an unclean thing, and all our righteousnesses are as filthy rags; and we all do fade as a leaf; and our iniquities, like the wind, have taken us away. Isaiah 64:6

Behold, the days come, saith the Lord, that I will raise unto David a righteous Branch, and a King shall reign and prosper, and shall execute judgment and justice in the earth. Jeremiah 23:5

Even the righteousness of God which is by faith of Jesus Christ unto all and upon all them that believe: for there is no difference. Romans 3:22

Whom God hath set forth to be a propitiation through faith in his blood, to declare his righteousness for the remission of sins that are past, through the forbearance of God; Romans 3:25

To declare, I say, at this time his righteousness: that he might be just, and the justifier of him which believeth in Jesus. Romans 3:26

For if by one man's offence death reigned by one; much more they which receive abundance of grace and of the gift of righteousness shall reign in life by one, Jesus Christ. Romans 5:17

Therefore as by the offence of one judgment came upon all men to condemnation; even so by the righteousness of one the free gift came upon all men unto justification of life. Romans 5:18

For as by one man's disobedience many were made sinners, so by the obedience of one shall many be made righteous. Romans 5:19

For they being ignorant of God's righteousness, and going about to establish their own righteousness, have not submitted themselves unto the righteousness of God.
For Christ is the end of the law for righteousness to every one that believeth. Romans 10:3,4

For he hath made him to be sin for us, who knew no sin; that we might be made the righteousness of God in him. 2 Corinthians 5:21

For by grace are ye saved through faith; and that not of yourselves: it is the gift of God: Ephesians 2:8

Let us therefore come boldly unto the throne of grace, that we may obtain mercy, and find grace to help in time of need. Hebrews 4:16

SANCTIFICATION

Speak thou also unto the children of Israel, saying, Verily my sabbaths ye shall keep: for it is a sign between me and you throughout your generations; that ye may know that I am the Lord that doth sanctify you. Exodus 31:13

Sanctify yourselves therefore, and be ye holy; for I am the Lord your God.
And ye shall keep my statutes, and do them: I am the Lord which sanctify you. Leviticus 20:7,8

Unto the church of God which is at Corinth, to them that are sanctified in Christ Jesus, called to be saints, with all that in every place call upon the name of Jesus Christ our Lord, both their's and our's: 1 Corinthians 1:2

Be ye not unequally yoked together with unbelievers: for what fellowship hath righteousness with unrighteousness? And what communion hath light with darkness?
And what accord hath Christ with Belial? Or what part hath he that believeth with an infidel?
And what agreement hath the temple of God with idols? For ye are the temple of the living God; as God hath said, I will dwell in them, and walk in them; and I will be their God, and they shall be my people.
Wherefore come out from among them, and be ye separate, saith the Lord, and touch not the unclean thing; and I will receive you,
And will be a Father unto you, and ye shall be my sons and daughters, saith the Lord Almighty. 2 Corinthians 6:14-18

Furthermore then we beseech you, brethren, and exhort you by the Lord Jesus, that as ye have received of us how ye ought to walk and to please God, so ye would abound more and more.
For ye know what commandments we gave you by the Lord Jesus.

For this is the will of God even your sanctification, that ye should abstain from fornication:
That every one of you should know how to possess his vessel in sanctification and honour;
Not in the lust of concupiscence, even as the Gentiles which know not God: 1 Thessalonians 4:1-5

And the very God of peace sanctify you wholly; and I pray God your whole spirit and soul and body be preserved blameless unto the coming of our Lord Jesus Christ. 1 Thessalonians 5:23

By the which will we are sanctified through the offering of the body of Jesus Christ once for all. Hebrews 10:10

SALVATION

The Lord shall fight for you, and ye shall hold your peace. Exodus 14:14

Ye shall not need to fight in this battle: set yourselves, stand ye still, and see the salvation of the Lord with you, O Judah and Jerusalem: fear not, nor be dismayed; to morrow go out against them: for the Lord will be with you. 2 Chronicles 20:17

My soul fainteth for thy salvation: but I hope in thy word. Psalm 119:81

I have longed for thy salvation, O Lord, and thy law is my delight. Psalm 119:174

Look unto me, and be ye saved, all the ends of the earth: for I am God, and there is none else. Isaiah 45:22

Rejoice greatly, O daughter of Zion! Shout, O daughter of Jerusalem! Behold your King is coming to you; He is just and having salvation;

Lowly and riding on a donkey, A colt, the foal of a donkey. Zechariah 9:9 NKJV

Therefore the Lord himself shall give you a sign; Behold, a virgin shall conceive, and bear a son, and shall call his name Immanuel. Isaiah 7:14

Now the birth of Jesus Christ was on this wise: When as his mother Mary was espoused to Joseph, before they came together, she was found with child of the Holy Ghost. Matthew 1:18

And she shall bring forth a son, and thou shalt call his name Jesus: for he shall save his people from their sins. Matthew 1:21

And knew her not till she had brought forth her first born son: and he called his name JESUS. Matthew 1:25

Come unto me, all ye that labour and are heavy laden, and I will give you rest.
Take my yoke upon you, and learn of me; for I am meek and lowly in heart: and ye shall find rest unto your souls.
For my yoke is easy, and my burden is light. Matthew 11:28-30

For this is my blood of the new testament, which is shed for many for the remission of sins. Matthew 26:28

And saying, The time is fulfilled, and the kingdom of God is at hand: repent ye, and believe the gospel. Mark 1:15

And hath raised up an horn of salvation for us in the house of his servant David; Luke 1:69

That we should be saved from our enemies, and from the hand of all that hate us. Luke 1:71

Strive to enter in at the straight gate: for many, I say unto you, will seek to enter in, and shall not be able. Luke 13:24

For God so loved the world, that he gave his only begotten Son, that whosoever believeth in him should not perish, but have everlasting life. John 3:16

For God sent not his Son into the world to condemn the world; but that the world through him might be saved. John 3:17

Jesus answered and said unto him, Verily, verily, I say unto thee, Except a man be born again, he cannot see the kingdom of God. John 3:3

Verily, verily, I say unto you, He that heareth my word, and believeth on him that sent me, hath everlasting life, and shall not come into condemnation; but is passed from death unto life. John 5:24

The thief cometh not, but for to steal, and to kill, and to destroy: I am come that they might have life, and that they might have it more abundantly. John 10:10

And I give unto them eternal life; and they shall never perish, neither shall any man pluck them out of my hand. John 10:28

Jesus saith unto him, I am the way, the truth, and the life: no man cometh unto the Father, but by me. John 14:6

And it shall come to pass, that whosoever shall call on the name of the Lord shall be saved. Acts 2:21

Repent ye therefore, and be converted, that your sins may be blotted out, when the times of refreshing shall come from the presence of the Lord; Acts 3:19

Neither is there salvation in any other: for there is none other name under heaven given among men, whereby we must be saved. Acts 4:12

But God commendeth his love toward us, in that, while we were yet sinners, Christ died for us. Romans 5:8

For as by one man's disobedience many were made sinners, so by the obedience of one shall many be made righteous. Romans 5:19

Much more then, being now justified by his blood, we shall be saved from wrath through him. Romans 5:9

That if thou shalt confess with thy mouth the Lord Jesus, and shalt believe in thine heart that God hath raised him from the dead, thou shalt be saved.
For with the heart man believeth unto righteousness: and with the mouth confession is made unto salvation. Romans 10:9,10

For by grace are ye saved through faith; and that not of yourselves: it is the gift of God: Ephesians 2:8

In whom ye also trusted, after that ye heard the word of truth, the gospel of your salvation: in whom also after that ye believed, ye were sealed with that holy Spirit of promise, Ephesians 1:13

Wherefore, my beloved, as ye have always obeyed, not as in my presence only, but now much more in my absence, work out your own salvation with fear and trembling. Philippians 2:12

For God hath not appointed us to wrath, but to obtain salvation by our Lord Jesus Christ,
Who died for us, that, whether we wake or sleep, we should live together with him. 1 Thessalonians 5:9,10

And being made perfect, he became the author of eternal salvation unto all them that obey him; Hebrews 5:9

The Lord is not slack concerning his promise, as some men count slackness; but is longsuffering to us-ward, not willing that any should perish, but that all should come to repentance. 2 Peter 3:9

Neither by the blood of goats and calves, but by his own blood he entered in once into the holy place, having obtained eternal redemption for us. Hebrews 9:12

But these are written, that ye might believe that Jesus is the Christ, the Son of God; and that believing ye might have life through his name. John 20:31

For there is one God, and one mediator between God and men, the man Christ Jesus; 1 Timothy 2:5

SPEAKING IN TONGUES

And I say unto you, Ask, and it shall be given you; seek, and ye shall find; knock, and it shall be opened unto you.
For every one that asketh receiveth; and he that seeketh findeth; and to him that knocketh it shall be opened. Luke 11:9,10

And when he had said this, he breathed on them, and saith unto them, Receive ye the Holy Ghost: John 20:22

For John truly baptized with water; but ye shall be baptized with the Holy Ghost not many days hence. Acts 1:5

And they were all filled with the Holy Ghost, and began to speak with other tongues, as the Spirit gave them utterance. Acts 2:4

For they heard them speak with tongues, and magnify God…Acts 10:46

For with stammering lips and another tongue will he speak to this people. Isaiah 28:11

And these signs shall follow them that believe; In my name shall they cast out devils; they shall speak with new tongues; Mark 16:17

And when Paul had laid his hands upon them, the Holy Ghost came on them, and they spake with tongues, and prophesied. Acts 19:6

For he that speaketh in an unknown tongue speaketh not unto men, but unto God: for no man understandeth him; howbeit in the spirit he speaketh mysteries. 1 Corinthians 14:2

He that speaketh in an unknown tongue edifieth himself;...1 Corinthians 14:4

For if I pray in an unknown tongue, my spirit prayeth, but my understanding is unfruitful. 1 Corinthians 14:14

Wherefore tongues are for a sign, not to them that believe, but to them that believe not:...1 Corinthians 14:22

But ye, beloved, building up yourselves on your most holy faith, praying in the Holy Ghost, Jude 20

SPIRIT OF THE ANTICHRIST

For such are false apostles, deceitful workers, transforming themselves into the apostles of Christ.
And no marvel; for Satan himself is transformed into an angel of light. Therefore it is no great thing if his ministers also be transformed as the ministers of righteousness; whose end shall be according to their works. 2 Corinthians 11:13-15

Little children, it is the last time: and as ye have heard that antichrist shall come, even now are there many antichrists; whereby we know that it is the last time. 1 John 2:18
Who is a liar but he that denieth that Jesus is the Christ? He is antichrist, that denieth the Father and the Son. 1 John 2:22

Beloved, believe not every spirit, but try the spirits whether they are of God: because many false prophets are gone out into the world.
Hereby know ye the Spirit of God: Every spirit that confesseth that Jesus Christ is come in the flesh is of God:
And every spirit that confesseth not that Jesus Christ is come in the flesh is not of God: and this is that spirit of antichrist, whereof ye have heard that it should come; and even now already is it in the world. 1 John 4:1-3

For many deceivers are entered into the world, who confess not that Jesus Christ is come in the flesh. This is a deceiver and an antichrist. 2 John 7

Whosoever transgresseth, and abideth not in the doctrine of Christ, hath not God. He that abideth in the doctrine of Christ, he hath both the Father and the Son.If there come any unto you, and bring not this doctrine, receive him not into your house, neither bid him God speed: For he that biddeth him God speed is partaker of his evil deeds. 2 John 9-11

TATTOOS

Ye shall not make any cuttings in your flesh for the dead, nor print any marks upon you: I am the Lord. Leviticus 19:28

TEMPTATION

Jesus said unto him, It is written again, Thou shalt not tempt the Lord thy God. Matthew 4:7

And lead us not into temptation, but deliver us from evil: For thine is the kingdom, and the power, and the glory, for ever. Amen. Matthew 6:13

Watch and pray, that ye enter not into temptation: the spirit indeed is willing, but the flesh is weak. Matthew 26:41

Defraud ye not one the other, except it be with consent for a time, that ye may give yourselves to fasting and prayer; and come together again, that Satan tempt you not for your incontinency. 1 Corinthians 7:5

There hath no temptation taken you but such as is common to man: but God is faithful, who will not suffer you to be tempted above that ye are able; but will with the temptation also make a way to escape, that ye may be able to bear it. 1 Corinthians 10:13

Brethren, if a man be overtaken in a fault, ye which are spiritual, restore such an one in the spirit of meekness; considering thyself, lest thou also be tempted. Galatians 6:1

But they that will be rich fall into temptation and a snare, and into many foolish and hurtful lusts, which drown men in destruction and perdition. 1 Timothy 6:9

For in that he himself hath suffered being tempted, he is able to succour them that are tempted. Hebrews 2:18

For we have not an high priest which cannot be touched with the feeling of our infirmities; but was in all points tempted like as we are, yet without sin. Hebrews 4:15

Let no man say when he is tempted, I am tempted of God: for God cannot be tempted with evil, neither tempteth he any man:
But every man is tempted, when he is drawn away of his own lusts and enticed. James 1:13,14

The Lord knoweth how to deliver the godly out of temptations, and to reserve the unjust unto the day of judgment to be punished: 2 Peter 2:9

My brethren, count it all joy when ye fall into divers temptations; James 1:2

Submit yourselves therefore to God. Resist the devil, and he will flee from you. James 4:7

TITHES AND OFFERINGS

And in process of time it came to pass, that Cain brought of the fruit of the ground an offering unto the Lord.
And Abel, he also brought of the firstlings of his flock and of the fat thereof. And the Lord had respect unto Abel and to his offering: Genesis 4:3,4

Speak unto the children of Israel, that they bring me an offering: of every man that giveth it willingly with his heart ye shall take my offering. Exodus 25:2

And all the tithe of the land, whether of the seed of the land, or of the fruit of the tree, is the Lord's: it is holy unto the Lord. Leviticus 27:30

Then there shall be a place which the Lord your God shall choose to cause his name to dwell there; thither shall ye bring all that I command you; your burnt offerings, and your sacrifices, your tithes, and the heave offering of your hand, and all your choice vows which ye vow unto the Lord. Deuteronomy 12:11

Every man shall give as he is able, according to the blessing of the Lord thy God which he hath given thee. Deuteronomy 16:17

That thou shalt take of the first of all the fruit of the earth, which thou shalt bring of thy land that the Lord thy God giveth thee, and shalt put it in a basket, and shalt go unto the place which the Lord thy God shall choose to place his name there. Deuteronomy 26:2

And as soon as the commandment came abroad, the children of Israel brought in abundance the firstfruits of corn, wine, and oil, and honey, and of all the increase of the field; and the tithe of all things brought they in abundantly. 2 Chronicles 31:5

And Azariah the chief priest of the house of Zadok answered him, and said, Since the people began to bring the offerings into the house of the Lord, we have had enough to eat, and have left plenty: for the Lord hath blessed his people; and that which is left is this great store. 2 Chronicles 31:10

Will a man rob God? Yet ye have robbed me. But ye say, Wherein have we robbed thee? In tithes and offerings.

Ye are cursed with a curse: for ye have robbed me, even this whole nation.

Bring ye all the tithes into the storehouse, that there may be meat in mine house, and prove me now herewith, saith the Lord of hosts, if I will not open you the windows of heaven, and pour you out a blessing, that there shall not be room enough to receive it.

And I will rebuke the devourer for your sakes, and he shall not destroy the fruits of your ground; neither shall your vine cast her fruit before the time in the field, saith the Lord of hosts.

And all nations shall call you blessed: for ye shall be a delightsome land, saith the Lord of hosts. Malachi 3:8-12

Moreover, because I have set my affections to the house of my God, I have of mine own proper good, of gold and silver, which I have given to the house of my God, over and above all that I have prepared for the holy house, 1 Chronicles 29:3

Then the people rejoiced, for that they offered willingly, because with perfect heart they offered willingly to the Lord: and David the king also rejoiced with great joy. 1 Chronicles 29:9

Take heed that ye do not your alms before men, to be seen of them: otherwise ye have no reward of your Father which is in heaven. Matthew 6:1

But when thou doest alms, let not thy left hand know what thy right hand doeth:
That thine alms may be in secret: and thy Father which seeth in secret himself shall reward thee openly. Matthew 6:3,4

Give, and it shall be given unto you; good measure, pressed down, and shaken together, and running over, shall men give into your bosom. For with the same measure that ye mete withal it shall be measured to you again. Luke 6:38

Upon the first day of the week let every one of you lay by him in store, as God hath prospered him, that there be no gatherings when I come. 1 Corinthians 16:2

But this I say, He which soweth sparingly shall reap also sparingly; and he which soweth bountifully shall reap also bountifully.
Every man according as he purposeth in his heart, so let him give; not grudgingly, or of necessity: for God loveth a cheerful giver. 2 Corinthians 9:6,7

Now he that ministereth seed to the sower both minister bread for your food, and multiply your seed sown, and increase the fruits of your righteousness. 2 Corinthians 9:10

THE TONGUE

I said, I will take heed to my ways, that I sin not with my tongue: I will keep my mouth with a bridle, while the wicked is before me. Psalm 39:1

I will bless the Lord at all times: his praise shall continually be in my mouth. Psalm 34:1

Keep thy tongue from evil, and thy lips from speaking guile. Psalm 34:13

And my tongue shall speak of thy righteousness and of thy praise all the day long. Psalm 35:28

The mouth of the righteous speaketh wisdom, and his tongue talketh of judgment. Psalm 37:30

Whoso privily slandereth his neighbour, him will I cut off: him that hath an high look and a proud heart will not I suffer. Psalm 101:5

The law of thy mouth is better unto me than thousands of gold and silver. Psalm 119:72

He that hideth hatred with lying lips, and he that uttereth a slander, is a fool.
In the multitude of words there wanteth not sin: but he that refraineth his lips is wise. Proverbs 10:18,19

The lips of the righteous know what is acceptable: but the mouth of the wicked speaketh frowardness. Proverbs 10:32

An hypocrite with his mouth destroyeth his neighbour: but through knowledge shall the just be delivered. Proverbs 11:9

The lip of truth shall be established forever: but a lying tongue is but for a moment. Proverbs 12:19

Whoso curseth his father or his mother, his lamp shall be put out in obscure darkness. Proverbs 20:20

Whoso keepeth his mouth and his tongue keepeth his soul from troubles. Proverbs 21:23

The tongue of the just is as choice silver: the heart of the wicked is little worth.
The lips of the righteous feed many: but fools die for want of wisdom. Proverbs 10:20,21

A wholesome tongue is a tree of life: but perverseness therein is a breach in the spirit. Proverbs 15:4

A man's belly shall be satisfied with the fruit of his mouth; and with the increase of his lips shall he be filled. Proverbs 18:20

Death and life are in the power of the tongue: and they that love it shall eat the fruit thereof. Proverbs 18:21

A fool's mouth is his destruction, and his lips are the snare of his soul. Proverbs 18:7

A lying tongue hateth those that are afflicted by it; and a flattering mouth worketh ruin. Proverbs 26:28

The north wind driveth away rain: so doth an angry countenance a backbiting tongue. Proverbs 25:23

Curse not the king, no not in thy thought; and curse not the rich in thy bedchamber: for a bird of the air shall carry the voice, and that which hath wings shall tell the matter. Ecclesiastes 10:20

Let no corrupt communication proceed out of your mouth, but that which is good to the use of edifying, that it may minister grace unto the hearers. Ephesians 4:29

Let your speech be alway with grace, seasoned with salt, that ye may know how ye ought to answer every man. Colossians 4:6

And that every tongue should confess that Jesus Christ is Lord, to the glory of God the Father. Philippians 2:11

If any man among you seem to be religious, and bridleth not his tongue, but deceiveth his own heart, this man's religion is vain. James 1:26

Even so the tongue is a little member, and boasteth great things Behold, how great a matter a little fire kindleth!
And the tongue is a fire, a world of iniquity: so is the tongue among our members, that it defileth the whole body, and setteth on fire the course of nature; and it is set on fire of hell. James 3:5,6

But the tongue can no man tame; it is an unruly evil, full of deadly poison.
Therewith bless we God, even the Father; and therewith curse we men, which are made after the similitude of God.
Out of the same mouth proceedeth blessing and cursing. My brethren, these things ought not so to be. James 3:8-10

For with the heart man believeth unto righteousness; and with the mouth confession is made unto salvation. Romans 10:10

TRUSTING GOD

Then said David to the Philistine, Thou comest to me with a sword, and with a spear, and with a shield: but I come to thee in the name of the Lord of hosts, the God of the armies of Israel, whom thou hast defied.
This day will the Lord deliver thee into mine hand; and I will smite thee, and take thine head from thee; and I will give the carcases of the hosts of the Philistines this day unto the fowls of the air, and to the wild beasts of the earth; that all the earth may know that there is a God in Israel.
And all this assembly shall know that the Lord saveth not with sword and spear: for the battle is the LORD'S, and he will give you into our hands. 1 Samuel 17:45-47

God is not a man, that he should lie; neither the son of man, that he should repent: hath he said, and shall he not do it? Or hath he spoken, and shall he not make it good? Numbers 23:19

But let all those that put their trust in thee rejoice: Let them ever shout for joy, because thou defendest them: let them also that love thy name be joyful in thee. Psalm 5:11

And they that know thy name will put their trust in thee: for thou, Lord, hast not forsaken them that seek thee. Psalm 9:10

Some trust in chariots, and some in horses: but we will remember the name of the Lord our God. Psalm 20:7

Our fathers trusted in thee: they trusted, and thou didst deliver them. They cried unto thee and were delivered: they trusted in thee, and were not confounded. Psalm 22:4,5

He trusted on the Lord that he would deliver him: let him deliver him, seeing he delighted in him. Psalm 22:8

O my God, I trust in thee: let me not be ashamed, let not mine enemies triumph over me. Psalm 25:2

Many sorrows shall be to the wicked: but he that trusteth in the Lord, mercy shall compass him about. Psalm 32:10

For our heart shall rejoice in him, because we have trusted in his holy name. Psalm 33:21

The Lord redeemeth the soul of his servants: and none of them that trust in him shall be desolate. Psalm 34:22

Trust in the Lord, and do good; so shalt thou dwell in the land, and verily thou shalt be fed. Psalm 37:3

For I will not trust in my bow, neither shall my sword save me. Psalm 44:6

Blessed is that man that maketh the Lord his trust, and respecteth not the proud, nor such as turn aside to lies. Psalm 40:4

In God have I put my trust: I will not be afraid what man can do unto me. Psalm 56:11

Trust in him at all times; ye people, pour out your heart before him: God is a refuge for us. Selah. Psalm 62:8

In thee, O Lord, do I put my trust: let me never be put to confusion. Psalm 71:1

But it is good for me to draw near to God: I have put my trust in the Lord God, that I may declare all thy works. Psalm 73:28

It is better to trust in the Lord than to put confidence in man. Psalm 118:8

It is better to trust in the Lord than to put confidence in princes. Psalm 118:9

Remember the word unto thy servant, upon which thou hast caused me to hope.
This is my comfort in my affliction: for thy word hath quickened me. Psalm 119:49,50

I will lift up mine eyes unto the hills, from whence cometh my help.
My help cometh from the Lord, which made heaven and earth. Psalm 121:1,2

Put not your trust in princes, nor in the son of man, in whom there is no help. Psalm 146:3

Trust in the Lord with all thine heart; and lean not unto thine own understanding. Proverbs 3:5

The name of the Lord is a strong tower: the righteous runneth into it, and is safe. Proverbs 18:10

Blessed is the man that trusteth in the Lord, and whose hope the Lord is. Jeremiah 17:7

…My little daughter lieth at the point of death: I pray thee, come and lay thy hands on her, that she may be healed; and she shall live. Mark 5:23

Blessed be the God and Father of our Lord Jesus Christ, who hath blessed us with all spiritual blessings in heavenly places in Christ: Ephesians 1:3

Now unto him that is able to do exceeding abundantly above all that we ask or think, according to the power that worketh in us. Ephesians 3:20

Let us hold fast the profession of our faith without wavering; (for he is faithful that promised;) Hebrews 10:23

In hope of eternal life, which God, that cannot lie, promised before the world began; Titus 1:2

WARFARE

And I will put enmity between thee and the woman, and between thy seed and her seed; it shall bruise thy head, and thou shalt bruise his heel. Genesis 3:15

No weapon that is formed against thee shall prosper; and every tongue that shall rise against thee in judgment thou shalt condemn. This is the heritage of the servants of the Lord, and their righteousness is of me, saith the Lord. Isaiah 54:17

These things have I spoken unto you, that in me ye might have peace. In the world ye shall have tribulation: but be of good cheer; I have overcome the world. John 16:33

What shall we then say to these things? If God be for us, who can be against us? Romans 8:31

The night is far spent, the day is at hand: let us therefore cast off the works of darkness, and let us put on the armour of light. Romans 13:12

Lest Satan should get an advantage of us: for we are not ignorant of his devices. 2 Corinthians 2:11

By the word of truth, by the power of God, by the armour of righteousness on the right hand and on the left, 2 Corinthians 6:7

For though we walk in the flesh, we do not war after the flesh:
(For the weapons of our warfare are not carnal, but mighty through God to the pulling down of strong holds;)
Casting down imaginations, and every high thing that exalteth itself against the knowledge of God, and bringing into captivity every thought to the obedience of Christ; 2 Corinthians 10:3-5

But let us, who are of the day, be sober, putting on the breastplate of faith and love; and for an helmet, the hope of salvation. 1 Thessalonians 5:8

Put on the whole armour of God, that ye may be able to stand against the wiles of the devil.
For we wrestle not against flesh and blood, but against principalities, against powers, against the rulers of the darkness of this world, against spiritual wickedness in high places.

Wherefore take unto you the whole armour of God, that ye may be able to withstand in the evil day, and having done all, to stand.
Stand therefore, having your lions girt about with truth, and having on the breastplate of righteousness;
And your feet shod with the preparation of the gospel of peace;
Above all, taking the shield of faith, wherewith ye shall be able to quench all the fiery darts of the wicked.
And take the helmet of salvation, and the sword of the Spirit, which is the word of God: Ephesians 6:11-17

Praying always with all prayer and supplication in the Spirit and watching thereunto with all perseverance and supplication for all saints; Ephesians 6:18

No man that warreth entangeth himself with the affairs of this life; that he may please him who hath chosen him to be a soldier. 2 Timothy 2:4

Be sober, be vigilant; because your adversary the devil, as a roaring lion, walketh about, seeking whom he may devour. 1 Peter 5:8

For whatsoever is born of God overcometh the world: and this is the victory that overcometh the world, even our faith.
Who is he that overcometh the world, but he that believeth that Jesus is the Son of God? 1 John 5:4,5

Ye are of God, little children, and have overcome them: because greater is he that is in you, than he that is in the world. 1 John 4:4

0-595-26507-3

Printed in the United Kingdom
by Lightning Source UK Ltd.
9403200001B